ENVIRONMENTAL ECONOMICS

ENVIRONMENTAL ECONOMICS

THOMAS D. CROCKER
University of California, Riverside

A. J. ROGERS III
University of Wisconsin, Milwaukee

THE DRYDEN PRESS, INC.
Hinsdale, Illinois

Printed in the United States of America
4 3 2 1   008   1 2 3 4 5 6 7 8 9

PREFACE

This book itself is short enough that any good-sized preface could easily overshadow the text. However, a couple of comments are in order. Like many of man's major concerns, the quality of the world around us no longer *has to be* something that "just happens." In the past, man has messed up his environment, but not to a sufficient degree to cause universal attention. This is no longer the case. Today all the countries of the world are experiencing difficulties in keeping their refuse from burying them.

The purpose of this presentation is to identify and specify the area of concern as objectively as possible. Without this operation, there is only rhetoric, and rhetoric just ain't gonna do the job! Second, environmental quality is viewed within the context of this country's economic system. Thus, the groundwork is laid for a rational attack in developing tools to perform the cleanup.

Because of some time problems, this preface has been written by one of the coauthors—Rogers, by name. Brother Crocker must be congratulated for putting up with my many quirks while writing this tome. It's amazing, but we both remain as good friends today as when the project started. Both of us have worked very hard to eliminate errors. Needless to say, however, should any errors remain, they are my coauthor's fault—not mine.

A. J. R. III

P.S. by Crocker

May I echo the sentiments of my good friend and coauthor, Professor Rogers, in all but the last sentence. This statement is so patently absurd as to make clarification unnecessary. Any errors remaining in the manuscript are clearly the result of the incompetence of my dunderheaded coauthor.

T. D. C.

CONTENTS

1
CHAPTER

The Philosophy of Crud

For several thousand years man has been sweating blood trying to improve his lot. There's been a lot of discussion about what "improved lot" really means; usually "improvement" for a given generation includes more goods and services than were available to its forebears. This improvement usually means increased control over the environment. Viewing the situation over several hundred (or thousand) years, we've really made it big! Recently, however, our noses have been rubbed—figuratively and literally—in some pretty dirty stuff. We're beginning to wonder if we've really been so smart after all. Have we somehow started a process that will sink all our goodies and the quality of life under a gigantic pile of crud? It is technologically possible to do just that, but will such a disaster occur? What can we, as individuals living in a very complex society, do to prevent the disaster? Lots of people have many different answers to these questions. The two of us are going to take you on a guided tour of some ideas behind these answers as viewed by economists. This little book is short enough so that the trip can't be *too* boring. Play the game for a while. You *may* find it interesting, even if you think our ideas stink.

Nature Boy	Decadent Materialist
◄─────────────────────────────────►	
(no crud)	(lots of crud)

Corollaries:

1. **Economic growth is bad.**

2. **Any tampering with natural states is deadly.**

3. **Man's acquisitive nature must be changed or strictly controlled.**

Figure 1.1   Naturalist Approach—Goodies or Gook?

One body of thought has become very popular today. It says, roughly, that "man" is made up of two basic, conflicting, and identifiable parts. One part is "natural"—in harmony with mother nature; this part wears the white hat. The other part is "economic." This part embodies the fat-cat instinct that makes people want to have an unnatural roof (not a cave) over their heads, clothes on their backs, food in their guts, and lots of other goodies besides. The thinking goes that these two characteristics of man are incompatible. They flat can't exist in the same world. If we're going to preserve nature, economic man has got to go; conversely, if we insist on the goodies, it's curtains for all the virgin beauties of this worldly life. This really overstates the philosophy; but the essence is there, and the essence isn't really very useful either as a view of man *or* as a means of getting insight into the environmental quality problem. (See Figure 1.1.)

Economists see man as a creature sufficiently· complex to

make such a simplistic division of his nature impossible, or at least not very useful. Economists are interested in one particular problem faced by man—scarcity. Until now, at least, the things (and situations) man has *wanted* have far exceeded the things he found he *could have.* This is the scarcity with which economists are concerned. If things (or situations) are desirable and scarce, then choices must be made. To get one thing, man must give up something else. These "things" we're talking about will be discussed in detail in Chapter 3; for now, just remember that *anything* or any "state of being" is included. It could be watching the sunset versus watching the six o'clock news on the boob-tube. (You can't do both with the same eyeballs at the same time unless your eyeballs are arranged in a rather peculiar fashion.) It can also be a society's choice between having goods of war or goods of peace. (By the way, what is a "society"? Think about it.) Since a picture is supposed to be worth a thousand words, let's see what we're talking about in pictorial form. Forgotten your high school geometry? Don't sweat it. We'll lead you by your pudgy little fists (figuratively of course) with such care and detail that you will think you're back in kindergarten. In Figure 1.2, we start with two lines (axes). One goes up and down (vertical axis) and the other goes across (horizontal axis). The two lines join at point o. The vertical axis represents *war stuff,* and the horizontal axis represents *peace stuff.* The farther up the war goods axis goes, the more war goods are available; the farther to the right the peace goods axis goes, the more peace goods are available.

Now, if you take any point upward and to the right of point o, you'll get combinations of war stuff and peace stuff. For example, point c represents war stuff in the amount of *oh and* peace stuff in the amount *oe.* Similarly, point d represents *og* of war material and *of* of peace products. Even point b represents a combination of war and peace goods. It represents *ob* of war stuff and zero of peace goods. Point a, of course, represents *oa* of peace goods and zero of war goods.

Now let's belt in some assumptions. Assume that the graph represents the American economy tomorrow morning at 10 o'clock. The economy will have a given number of working

3

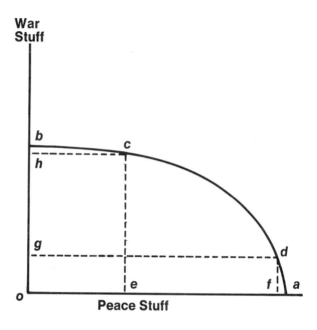

Figure 1.2   Production Possibilities

bodies, of factories, of machines, of known natural resources, and so on. Given this level of resources, the economy has some choices. If it devotes *all* these resources to war production, we'll assume *ob* of war goods can be produced, with zero peace production. If it devotes *all* its resources to peace production, we'll assume *oa* of peace stuff can be produced, with zero war production. It can also split up its resource use into some peace stuff and some war stuff. Points *c* and *d* represent such options. If all these options are plotted, we arrive at some *production possibilities* curve such as *bcda*. This curve represents a *boundary* between choices that are *possible* for society and choices that are *not possible,* given the full employment of all resources available at that time.

Points upward and to the right of *bcda* cannot be attained; points downward and to the left of *bcda* are possible. However, if society isn't operating on the boundary (if it's operating inside or to the left), either there will be unemployment of some resources or resources are being used inefficiently. This

4

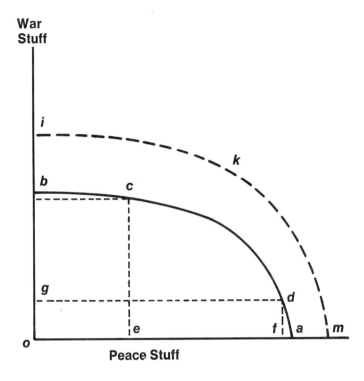

Figure 1.3   Production Possibilities

merely means that more of one product can be produced without reducing the production of the other. If the economy is at
full employment and all resources are being used efficiently
(operating somewhere on the boundary), the only way to get
more of one product is to give up some of the other.

Of course, if the available resources increase or if we find
a more efficient way of putting them together (better technology), our whole production possibilities boundary can be
shifted upward to the right, as in Figure 1.3. Now it is possible
to have more of one good *without* giving up production of the
other one. This is *one* way of describing economic growth.
(There *are* better ways.)

The economist, then, doesn't view man as something that
is necessarily going to foul up the entire ecological system of
his environment. He *does* view man as a being capable of

making choices. In most cases, man is also capable of changing many of his choices as different information becomes available about the potential results of alternative actions. The remaining chapters of this book will be devoted to explaining what the implications of these statements are as far as the quality of environment is concerned. Before leaving this chapter, however, we shall say a bit more about our friends who insist that man must be split into the good guy of nature and the bad guy of economic grubbing.

Natural scientists and many students of the humanities often accept the view that the "welfare of man" is primarily dependent upon how "good" the natural states around him are. The words in quotes are often used but seldom defined or quantified. Nature is the big mother of all things past and present. She has only limited ways of adjusting to change without completely screwing up the overall ecology. Equilibriums in which no overwhelming forces tend to change things may exist for the economic man *or* the natural man, but the two cannot coexist. Imagine all the different ecological systems that have existed on the North American continent from, say, 1066 A.D. until today. We go from the noble savages of old doing their thing with carefree abandon to the United States Army Corps of Engineers doing God knows *whose* thing.

If we line up all the systems of history from the most natural to the most "man-made," our nature lovers will tend to favor those systems toward the natural end of the line. This preference doesn't necessarily result from a carefully reasoned conclusion based on the study of man's political, social, economic, and moral tendencies. Instead, it is an article of faith, a social value judgment that may very well conflict with values of other people—values such as freedom, justice, material progress, health, companionship, enlightenment, and peace. This position leads to a general hatred of anything tending to destroy or to deteriorate the natural states.

Another facet of this philosophy is that any destruction of a natural endowment will *reduce* man's options forever. The use of water or air for waste disposal, the construction of a freeway past a scenic view, the abandonment of the family farm—any act or happening that moves away from the "more natural" end of the possible ecosystems is bad news for all time. Population increases? Good grief! These upcoming bods are like maggots ready to feed on the soon-to-be-dead cow. Economic growth (often wrongfully equated with satisfying lustful, material pleasures of the flesh) tears some resources from the environment and fouls up those which remain. Private property and individualistic philosophies generate acts that do not respect the present generation or future generations. All these ideas are based on the assumption that society is organized to *dominate* nature rather than to *accommodate to* nature. The present organization of human purposes is based on neglect, ignorance, and/or callousness toward the world of nature that borders on moral decadence. Society is composed of individualistic arsonists who act only in their self interest and burn down their own pads to collect the fire insurance from the fat cat. When they are done with the burning, they find that the fat cat has died in the collective flames and there's nothing left to pay anyone anything. Governments don't help much, even "socialist" governments, because they're really nothing but tools of the arsonists anyway.

Of course, the above presentation represents an extreme position. Those who conceive of the split man have understood a fundamental truth. In some respects, man's ability to change his environment has advanced more rapidly than his ability to comprehend and calculate the implications of these changes for himself. Knocking out the overstatement, however, many responsible persons favor "more natural" ecological systems. They worry about apparent trends toward a civilization consisting of many billions of people, synthetic foods, and continents half covered with multistoried concrete structures. They feel that maybe man isn't as smart as he thinks he is. Man's monkeying around may upset ma nature to a point that the old girl herself, with or without man's help, will never be able to maintain life.

Nature without man's interference is vastly diversified. The diversity tends to give both stability and ability to adjust should circumstances change. After a disturbance, original conditions tend to return as if the biological community and the things associated with it had memories of what existed before. On the other hand, man establishes artificial and simplified communities, because such communities require less effort (in the broadest sense) to obtain a given quantity of output. Consider, for example, the completely managed forest (tree farm) with its row upon row of identically aged trees of a single species. This is a very efficient way of raising trees. The simplicity of the forest's organization, however, makes it highly susceptible to disease and to exploitation by other life forms. Man maintains this economically fruitful, but ecologically unstable, simplicity by frequent spraying, clearing, and nutritional programs. Many of these programs, for example, pesticide use, introduce artificial elements into the environment which drastically alter other natural systems. The effects on man are unpredictable, except that more artificiality must often be generated to deal with them.

The naturalist and the economist agree on one point. Man might harm himself or others because he does not possess enough accurate information about the impact of his actions. Also, he may not fully understand the information he does have. This may very well lead to decisions that are neither economically efficient nor morally desirable for society. It is possible that modification of socioeconomic structures could improve the information available to the decision maker. The economist, however, goes one step further in pointing out that information generally *is not a free good.* One must give up something to get information or to get better information. This *cost* consideration must also be thrown into the equation before pat answers such as "improved information" are suggested.

In 1865, a character by the name of W. Stanley Jevons published a little book called *The Coal Question.* The main idea of the book was that England was running out of coal. Coal had fueled her industrial revolution; therefore there was nothing ahead but doom and industrial death. As is too often the case with economists' predictions, events proved Jevons wrong. His sour view of the future was an extension of another view set forth earlier in the same century by Parson Malthus. This good reverend said that the stock of the earth's resources was fixed and that human populations would increase at geometric rates $(2 \times 2 \times 2 \ldots,$ not just $2 + 2 + 2 \ldots)$ until some big die-off

8

occurred. Sooner or later all men would have to live at bare subsistence levels and no more. While population increases are a recognized problem today, both Malthus and Jevons proved to be wrong in their predictions.

A few decades after Jevons's predictions of doom, a group of U.S.A.-type citizens picked up a new variation on this theme. This group, which sometimes included Teddy Roosevelt, asserted that if economic growth is not stopped *and* stopped *quickly,* our *stocks* of mineral and timber resources will be used up quickly and our industrial life will die of starvation. Seventy or eighty years later, not only have the stocks not been exhausted, but in most instances their costs are also less than they were in the earlier period. No one is suggesting that the problems of conservation raised by the doomsday predictors were not or are not perfectly valid. Because of better information and technology, we are better able today to cut down the "waste" of these resources than was the case in 1900. It's possible that these improvements were speeded up by the propaganda of the doomsday prophets, but the generalized solution suggested by them has *not* been adopted. For some of them, stopping all forms of economic growth would have been the only true solution to the problem of limited resource stocks.

Now we have a new generation of doomsday artists. Again, it's a slightly different variation, but the theme is the same. Pollution is taking over the earth! What do we do about it? Obviously, stop economic growth. It's the filthy factories and the smoke-belching automobiles that cause all the problems. Madison Avenue talks people into using throw-away containers. Don't blame the poor people who prefer the convenience of nonreturnables. It's all the problem of screwed-up values. Unless we get rid of this crass materialism, we've had the course.

The gloom pushers see two ways of changing this value system. The first of these is to change the nature of man by moral and gentle persuasion. The idea is to get man to prefer ecological systems closer to the natural states. If this doesn't work, get out the whip and force man to accept that ecology the "experts" say is right. As a long-run solution to any problem, the whip of repression of human wills has been something less than successful. Nevertheless, repression *should* be recognized as one alternative means of improving environmental quality.

On the other hand, the gentle moral suasion method (the for-God's-sake method) has had a good reputation as a means of improving the environment and mitigating scarcity throughout man's history. Whether by intention or not, a religion which emphasizes asceticism and contemplation reduces the strain man places on the environment. The dropout who wants only to contemplate cosmic forces and navels probably won't be particularly turned on by gunning a motorcycle over a forest green. He'll probably be something less than wild about guzzling beer in front of the idiot window watching "Gunsmoke." The whole idea is to search for peace with nature rather than to overcome the constraints imposed on man by nature. Ideally, man's interactions with his environment would be those of a well-behaved animal. Any increased output of goods and services would be dependent largely on uncontrolled natural forces.

Talk of persuading man to change his preferences in a drastic manner seems to be a rather forlorn basis on which to pin the medallion of environmental reform. Though establishing ideals may well be necessary for the long-term betterment of man, immediate results are likely to be comparatively unfruitful. Similarly, drastic efforts to restrict man's desires run up against other ideals. For example, an effort to prohibit piling up a junked car in a homeowner's yard runs up against the idea of a man's using his property as he sees fit. Some hold that freedom and justice—whatever they might be—can exist only in a society where great reliance is placed on respect for private property. Whatever the case, it is certainly true that attempts to restrict what a man is permitted to do often run afoul of notions that are among the strongest of Western civilizations. Thus, neither gentle suasion nor sledgehammers seem to hold much hope as viable policies to "improve our lot."

Both the persuasion and the force schools of thought have as their goal the restraint of economic growth and uninhibited market judgments, both of which are depicted as overcoming and overwhelming the natural world instead of accommodating to it. *Given the objective of maintaining the natural environ-*

10

ment, this suggested means may be sadly and badly misplaced. That is, given the wants that most people seem to have, *restraining* economic growth and *reducing* the place of market judgments *may worsen* rather than improve the state of the natural world.

There are at least three reasons for this. Economic *growth* and increases in real per capita incomes go hand in hand. (Notice we're not talking about economic improvement in a country and real per capita incomes being tied together. Fancy accounting at the national level can make this last relation as ridiculous as great-grandfather at a love-in. It can have more appearance than substance.) Thus, those who see a direct relation between pollutant levels (loadings) and economic growth must also observe the similar relation between pollutant loadings and increasing per capita incomes. Historically, increases in per capita income and increases in environmental pollutant loadings have tended to be *associated.* This does not mean that they are *necessarily related.*

Potential pollutant loadings and real per capita incomes are undoubtedly related. Economic growth usually involves the expanded use of materials previously unused and capable of generating pollution. But when the problem is stripped of all extraneous factors, *higher* per capita incomes and *reduced* pollutant loadings can tend to go hand in hand (are complementary)—instead of the popularly accepted contrary position (a competitive relation). Follow closely and you'll see why.

Imagine that man's wants are arranged in an order ranging from greatest to least. This ordering is based on how much of his resources man is willing to expend to obtain the particular want. There's little question that the highest place in this ordering would go to basic and fundamental biological wants—the subsistence needs for food, clothing, and shelter. As the highest priority wants are satisfied or partially satisfied, priorities will change and wants that were previously lower in the scale will increase in relative value. Lower order wants move up, and higher order wants move down, in terms of the resources man is now willing to expend. If I must choose between two equally attractive homesites, I will select that site which is *not* downwind from the local fertilizer plant. However, if the choice is between starving while living in an idyllic and pollution-free setting, and having wholesome food and adequate shelter while living near the factory chimney, most of us would choose the latter. We probably wouldn't be satisfied with our lot, but that's nothing new. Of course, this choice would be even more obvious if the smokey factory happened to be the place where we earned the bread to buy our food and to pay for our shelter. It's bloody hard to feed one's soul if the body doesn't get some kind of care and feeding first. Once the old bod has its physiological requirements taken care of, then soul feeding can commence to whatever degree is desired. In fact, it's close to certain not only that resources spent on feeding the soul will increase as available personal resources (real incomes) increase, but also that the percentage of incomes spent on soul feeding will increase. That makes soul feeding what the economists call a *superior economic good.* As real incomes increase, the percentage of total income spent on the good increases. Reducing pollution is certainly soul food. It may be required for life itself, but minimally we can expect more resources, both relatively and absolutely, to be spent on pollution control as per capita incomes increase. A further implication that can be expected from this reasoning is that the demand for cleanliness will *probably* go up faster than the demand for most other goods and services. In other words, the demand for a clean environment will probably go up faster than the demand for the goodies whose production increases pollutant loadings. A higher state of cleanliness *can be achieved* when real per capita incomes are high than when they are low. Cleanliness is next to affluence? (Sorry about that.)

Even if a negative relation existed between economic growth and environmental quality, the operation of an uninhibited market would tend to alleviate the negative impact to some degree. A reduction in the physical availability of a good means that the good is economically scarcer. As you will see in Chapter 3, "scarcer" means that market price will increase. Increased market price will reduce the quantity of the good used.

For example, assume the "good" in question consists of the psychic joys of camping in a virgin forest. If the use of the forest is "free" (It never will be, you know; the time spent there will have some alternative value and it usually takes resources just to get to camper heaven.), one can expect the use of the forest to reflect this apparent abundance. If "use" means that some aspect of the forest is destroyed or depreciated, the destruction or depreciation will occur at a much higher rate under conditions of zero cost than would be the case if people had to pay a price for the use. The higher the price, the lower the expected use; therefore, depreciation and destruction would be reduced. In simple terms, people won't be messing up the woods as much if the cost to them of being in the woods is raised.

This cost increase caused by pollution has another impact. Increased costs mean that incentives have increased to find substitutes for polluted resources and/or means for cleaning up these resources. Without this market incentive, the search for substitutes and technological innovations would be seriously curtailed. For example, the market, after observing the increased cost of providing beautiful forests, will seek cheaper ways of picking up tourist litter and/or accelerating the forest regeneration (self-destruct containers?). The free market operation provides inducements essential to the improvement of environmental quality. If the market operation is inhibited in such a way as to prevent the initial rise in costs, private attempts to alleviate the quality problem will be severely hindered if not eliminated.

Economic growth can aid the cause of clean environment in another way. It can raise real per capita incomes. These increased incomes mean that acquiring any particular good will involve giving up a *relatively* smaller portion of one's income than was previously required. For our problem, pollution control requires the expenditure of both material resources and human effort. Increased incomes mean that this expenditure may easily become a smaller proportion of total expenditures. Therefore, the real costs in terms of forgone alternatives *decreases* as economic growth causes real income to *increase.*

Every bit of available evidence indicates that innovation and technological change are intimately tied to economies experiencing comparatively rapid rates of growth and income increase. They are also tied to increased levels of wealth in an economy—wealth both in terms of physical capital stocks (machines, factories, and so on) and of human capital stocks (educated citizens) as well. Technological advance is an integral part of the growth process, because stocks of knowledge, far from being depleted by the process, expand geometrically. Every cost-reducing innovation opens up possibilities of application in many new directions, including maintenance or improvement of environmental quality. Attempts to restrain growth because of its supposed association with environmental deterioration may kill the one best hope of improving the situation. Restraining growth in the present generation may impose tremendous burdens on future generations as they continue the battle for better quality of life. Lower growth *now* means lower capital stocks in the *future.* Lower capital stocks make any endeavor, including pollution control, more difficult. If you find this concept difficult to accept, consider what the environmental quality might be if today's population were living with the technology of the 1850s. On the other hand, you might also like to compare the dung-ridden, fly-swollen, open-sewered, rat- and louse-infested cities of the 1850s with our far-from-ideal cities of today.

It must be reemphasized that there can be two types of disagreement about what constitutes "desirable" natural states. The first is a question of values and nothing more. Some people prefer "more natural" states than do others. The objectives in life of each group differ. It may well be that those who prefer natural states do not at the moment have their preferences accurately registered in the market. That is, the market does not properly weigh their preferences. For this problem, the answer is to structure the market in such a way as to give their preferences proper weight.

The second type of disagreement arises not because of differences in objectives but because of differences in the means by which these objectives can best be met. For example, the ecologist and the economist might agree that the objective is to provide man with the maximum opportunity to do his thing. They may disagree on the best means to pull it off. The ecologist predicts disaster if we pollute our rivers. The economist points out that clean-up of rivers costs resources that could be used to feed the poor. If the two agreed on the effects, they would probably agree on policies. The difference is not a moral one but a scientific one.

None of the preceding discussion is meant to imply that concern for the present state of our environment is without foundation. Clearly the wants of the extreme conservationists cannot nor should not be ignored. Most people, however, are probably not prepared to live the pure, simple, but rugged life they suggest. Similarly, we can't ignore the wants of the extreme "free enterpriser," who brooks no interference with his business. However, we can't live with all the results of his wants when these include grossly polluted air and water and a generally uncomfortable life. The real question, of course, is *why* doesn't this beautiful market system of ours prevent the problem in the first place? Even worse, given that we have the problem, how come the bloody system doesn't correct it? These are the questions we will be addressing ourselves to from now until you hit the back cover of this book. The problem is twofold (and we suspect the naturalist cats will agree). There are values in the society that the market is missing completely. They just don't seem to get into the measurement process at all. And then there are those values which markets may distort for a variety of reasons. These problems we readily admit, and our purpose is to analyze them in a reasonably basic way. With the voice of revolt abroad in the land today, many feel that the whole damn system is wrong and should be dumped. We'll tell you right now that we disagree with that position. All we're asking is your consideration of our analyses and suggestions. We feel that to dump the system is to throw the baby out with the bath water, and that's an expensive way to do business (particularly for the baby). Obviously, the system needs some calibration or correction in certain areas. We'll look at some of the options.

Our purpose here is to show that ecological disaster need not necessarily come to pass with a reasonably free operation of the market and with economic growth. We will proceed to present the basic economics of environmental quality and to show ways of correcting the operation of the market so that all relevant values can be recorded and weighed. Our task in

15

the next chapter is to present some of the physical and technological aspects of our topic necessary for an understanding of the economic analysis and examples of the succeeding chapters.

2
CHAPTER

Materials Balance

In this chapter we discuss some physical systems involved in our problem. We look at what's going on and what some of the potential choices might be in reducing the impact of the pollution problem. In the following chapters we will discuss the *economics* of these choices. Now, let's just identify man's alternatives in the light of the physical and technical world in which he lives.

Our universe can be viewed as a gigantic bundle of resources. (See Figure 2.1.) At any moment, this bundle is fixed, although man in his wisdom doesn't know what that fixed amount is. For example, we're still discovering petroleum deposits; one hundred years ago nobody really knew what to do with the black junk. Our idea of what constitutes a useful resource changes rapidly. Anyway, man takes these resources and converts them into things from which he derives services. Using these products results in something that can be called *utility*. If you'd rather call it happiness or satisfaction or well-being or something similar, be our guest. Whatever the word, man likes the use of these products. To *produce* them and/or to *use* them generates something more than just utility. It also generates junk or garbage, or crud of one kind or another. Hopefully, this crud can be converted *back* into a reusable

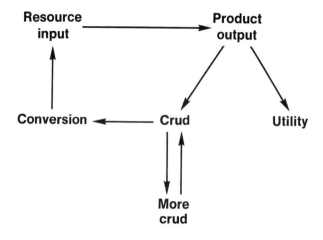

Figure 2.1   Materials Balance

resource without upsetting anyone in the process. If this happens, we can start all over again.

Unfortunately, the crud may collect on the side of the cycle and bother a lot of people. In fact, it can start a fine little vicious cycle of its own whereby a little crud to begin with can generate a little more crud, which contributes to the increase of the first batch, and on and on and on. Detergents in our waters may make the waters unpleasant to smell, taste, or look at. The phosphates in the detergents may go even further. They can provide the nutrients for all that beautiful green slime (algae) which further fouls up the water (unless you've got a real thing for green slime). Here, then, is the most general framework of the "big picture." It's so big and so general that a great deal is hidden, so a more detailed look is in order.

First of all, how *can* man use the natural environment in which he lives? That is, what materials or services can this environment yield?

The natural environment is an asset capable of perpetuating itself with or without man's help. Man derives *materials* and *services* from this environment. Coal is gouged from the hills of Kentucky. Land is paved to provide highways for communication—paved, incidentally, with materials gouged from another hillside. The poet, or even slobs like us, gains aesthetic pleasure and even spiritual renewal from a walk through the forest wilderness in Washington's Olympic Peninsula. Mayor Daley's little hamlet takes water from Lake Michigan, dumps the crud of humans and factories into this water, and then uses the Illinois River to carry Chicago's filth to the sea via the Mississippi River. The hiker will have little if any effect on the forest's ability to perpetuate itself (assuming he pays attention to Smokey the Bear). The breather of air in the great outdoors has little impact on the air's ability to provide breath for others. The acts of Mayor Daley's citizens and of the Kentucky strip miners *can* and *do* influence nature's ability to perpetuate the existing environment. Hillsides devoid of foliage or topsoil can become eroded deserts incapable of supporting vegetation. They also look like hell to most people. The Illinois River certainly isn't much for sport fishing, but it does have one advantage. If you fall in, you'll be able to walk to shore without benefit of life jacket or the Holy Ghost. It's slippery, but solid!

At this point, we can all gnash our teeth, beat our breasts, and curse at the s.o.b.'s in Chicago and Kentucky that make the world an unfit place to live. *Hold it!* The coal from the hillside provides some cheap fuel which keeps kids in the ghetto from freezing to death in the winter. Okay, so it also generates some juice to light a Coca Cola sign all night. Nevertheless, man *gains* and loses at the same time. There is a trade-off between the aesthetics of the rolling hill and the products of energy. What happens if Chicago doesn't dump its crud into the Illinois? Well, it could use Lake Michigan and destroy one of the most valuable bodies of fresh water in the world. It could also retrieve and dry all the solid stuff. This could then be burned (and increase smog in the area) or be hauled away by truck or rail to build some new "mountains" in southern Wisconsin.

The strip-mining and the sanitary-sewer cases illustrate the two types of action by which man alters the potential materials and services available in the natural environment. In the strip-mining case, the environment is altered when man *removes* a resource for uses valuable to him. In the sanitary-sewer case, the environment is altered because of efforts to get rid of materials nobody wants. The valuable resource in the latter case is the river's ability to transport, dilute, and assimilate waste materials. In spite of the apparent differences in the two examples, they are formally similar. Each case involves an alteration in the materials and services that the environment is capable of yielding in any given time interval. Most importantly, this alteration can be avoided *only* if:

1. We cut down production of the goodies or the crud; *or*
2. We find other technologies to produce the goodies with less crud; *or*
3. We find other means of waste disposal less objectionable to man and the environment.

For example, we can let the kids in the ghetto shiver all winter. We might send them to Miami Beach (boy, would *that* shake up the troops!). For the sewage problem, we may be able to convince the good citizens of Chicago to eat less food and thus reduce the amount of human dung dumped into the drainage canal. Milwaukee takes sewage solids and produces a lawn and garden fertilizer. The only hooker with this program is that human manure is *very* low in chemical nutrients beneficial to plants. The thing that makes Milwaukee's process economical is the presence of brewery wastes which raise the quality of the fertilizer to a marketable level. The beers that made Milwaukee famous also make its fertilizer product worth handling.

Given present production processes, the total amount of waste products our consumption and production activities will release into the natural environment over some time period cannot be changed greatly. That is, the total tonnage of waste generated by a modern industrial civilization will not vary greatly, whatever the resources used. Of course, the *form* of the waste materials can differ substantially. Sooner or later, temporarily or permanently, *everything* becomes waste. By one route or another, what is taken from the natural environment must ultimately return. Ashes to ashes and dust to dust. All wastes are and always have been recycled, though the form any particular cycle takes may or may not include the natural

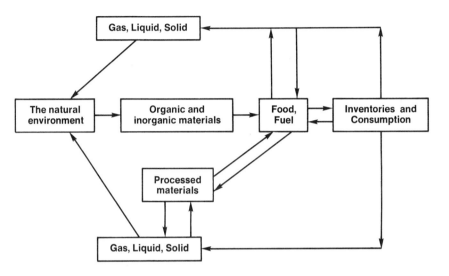

Figure 2.2 Resource Use and Return

environment. The waste problem and the environmental quality problem *are not caused by an absence of recycling.* The problems *are* caused by types of recycling which temporarily or permanently alter existing states of the natural environment. Man has many choices available to him regarding the types of recycling processes he employs. The problem is to find *in each instance* the recycle form which best suits *all* his purposes.

Figure 2.2 presents a more specific diagram of the several interactions between nature and man's activities. We are still dealing with a highly generalized analysis which completely omits the different impacts of specific waste materials returned to the natural environment. It should be explicitly recognized that the *form* of wastes generated from the use of a natural resource may vary depending greatly on the use made of the resource.

Consider, for example, two products of crude oil. Chlorinated hydrocarbon insecticides are one category of products derived from crude oil. Probably the most notorious of these products is DDT. This chemical is so persistent that it can accumulate over several generations in the tissues, fats, and reproductive organs of plants and animals. It is probable that sufficient accumulations can cause mutations which may change the form of life itself. Another product of crude oil is gasoline, which is burned in automobiles and discharges combustion by-products into the atmosphere. These harmful gases can again affect life processes by being ingested into the respiratory systems of living things. Thus it is that the raw product, crude oil, can be used to produce very different consumption products which in turn produce vastly different waste forms. The impact on the natural environment can also differ greatly.

Figure 2.2 illustrates an important facet of the whole cycling problem. We are facing a two-state decision. The first state involves the decision whether to consume at all. No joke! This decision is implicit anytime we do anything that takes from nature some element for our use. If we decide to *really* give nature a break, we will no longer take anything at all from our environment. Within a very short period, the whole problem will be solved, because man himself will no longer be around to screw up nature's playground.

On the other hand, assuming the first-order decision to consume is made, our problem becomes that of which cycles to choose in the production-consumption-waste operations. As the diagram indicates, we take from the environment and use materials for food and fuel. The consumption and production processes generate waste which will be (1) recycled back through the natural environment or (2) short-circuited back through the production processes themselves.

This choice has tremendous implications for the whole environmental quality question, as can be shown in a few simple examples. The inputs of the system are the organic and the inorganic materials removed from the natural environment. Only those materials singly or jointly capable of providing man with valuable services are removed. The leftovers are returned to nature. Take trees as an example. Trees are cut and processed to make paper, fuel, lumber, and chemicals. Sometimes the process includes returning directly to the natural environment waste products such as tree bark and sawdust (in many cases these by-products are also processed into valuable forms). Take the cycle of one of these products—paper. Paper is consumed in the form of throw-away containers, books, and many other goods. It is *physically possible* to collect and reprocess *all* waste paper so that none of it is returned to the natural environment. In other words, the cycle goes from processing to consumption back to processing and back again to consumption. What if some of it is *not* reprocessed but is flipped out on the highways or flushed down a toilet? Whether the waste paper is burned or decomposed by other processes in nature, the result will be a form no longer readily reconvertible to usable paper. The same chemicals exist in the products of decomposition, but reconversion into paper would be difficult and expensive.

Sooner or later *all* products return to the natural environment, but as can be seen by this closed-system analysis, recycling waste products by short-circuiting the natural environment can have two major beneficial effects. First, the total resources required from nature to maintain a given level of production is *reduced* by short circuiting. Second, the impact of the waste on the natural environment is reduced, since less of it is cycled through the environment. It must be emphasized that the reuse of waste materials without passing through the natural environment *is the key* to the reduction of the total tonnage of wastes placed in this environment during any particular time interval.

Without recycling, attempts to reduce wastes released into one medium will immediately increase wastes placed in another medium. For example, waste fibers from the production of paper can be discharged into a watercourse as a liquid. An alternative is to incinerate the fibers, thus creating a stench (gaseous pollution) you wouldn't believe. A third option is to dispose of the fibers in their initial solid form. This action will make some piece of property look like the devil except to insects and other pests, who will have a field day.

Another example of the interdependence of waste flows

is the common municipal incinerator. An "antipollution" device, called a wet scrubber, which can be attached to the incinerator, uses water sprays to trap, absorb, and remove particulate matter and gases from the combustion products of the incinerator. If more particulate material is to be removed, larger quantities of water will be required and more solid residues will be obtained for disposal by other means. The scrubbing water accumulates crud too, and getting rid of this mucky water may be just as serious a disposal problem as the original garbage. If one assumes

1. a given level of economic activity producing goods and services,
2. a given efficiency in producing goods and services,
3. a given level of waste recovery and recycling,

then reduction of one waste type can come only at the expense of creating another type. If appropriate equipment and energy are applied, *all* undesirable substances *can be* removed from air and water streams. But removed to where? The solid junk that will be left over must find a home somewhere, and that may pose an equally serious problem for the waste disposer.

Our simple schematic in Figure 2.2 shows another way in which waste materials can be reduced, in addition to increased recycling. Production and consumption processes that require smaller raw material *throughputs* will also reduce the waste products dumped back on nature. Take one of our best polluters as an example. Automobiles are generally driven by internal combustion engines. The bigger the bloody engine, the more gasoline consumed per time unit (or distance covered). The more gas consumed, the more combustion waste products generated. How come we all don't just get smaller cars with smaller engines? This would be cheaper for each of us and would save society many headaches (literally). The answer can be found in analyzing just what an automobile is, and better yet, just what an automobile *does*. Most of us will agree that autos provide transportation services. If "transportation services" were a homogeneous product (the same thing from all sources to all people), the problem would be simpler. Unfortunately, "transportation services" is almost meaningless unless we add other parameters. Here are just a few:

1. Transportation at what rates of speed?
2. Transportation over what distances?
3. Transportation at what times (hours of the day, seasons, and so on)?
4. Transportation at what level of creature comfort?
5. Transportation for how many at any one time?

Obviously, many more factors can change the whole meaning of our "service" definition. This is bad enough, but we have barely begun! Now add some of the other services yielded by automobiles, and we really have a mess. Sophisticated, educated, omniscient *you* (and we, of course) know damn well that the great gob of chrome hauled around on the latest Detroit product isn't worth the powder to blow it to hell. Fair enough. However, if Mr. Jones thinks it's cool, and Mr. Smith likes Mr. Jones's taste, both Jones and Smith will probably buy the bloody gob of chrome. The extra fifty horsepower needed to lug the goody may burn an extra couple of gallons of gas per hour, but that's only one drop in a big ocean that nobody will notice anyway. True enough for Jones and Smith, but Jones and Smith times several million produces a Los Angeles on a hot, still summer day. For heaven's sake, don't just blame the knotheads on Madison Avenue who convinced Jones and Smith they needed the junk. For every sucker*or*, there's got to be a sucker*ee*. If you think your tastes are so far superior to Jones's and Smith's, you'd better be a good salesman or have a helluva big stick.

Another example of reduced throughputs can be found if people are willing to buy larger unit packages of food and beverage. The material needed to make a one-gallon bottle is much less than that required for eight pint bottles or four quart jugs. Not long ago anyone who bought less than one bushel of apples at a crack was looked upon as being a little strange. A big purchase today is a four-pound cellophane bag; and for some of those tree-ripened beautiful big red hunks of dampened sawdust from the wild West, one apple at a time may be a major expenditure. Should we go back to the good old wooden bushel basket? Maybe, but let's look at some of the facets of this deal.

First of all, time will be expended by both buyer and seller in concluding a sale of apples. The buyer's time will probably be the same regardless of the size of the sale. The seller's time will be the same too *if* friendly John in the neighborhood grocery around the corner is personally selling you the cellophane bag or bushel. This is hardly ever the case today. Mr. A and Mr. P have gobbled up most of the friendly little independent grocers to line the pockets of their fat-cat stockholders with the exploitative profits derived from our hard-earned food dollar. Those friendly little surviving grocers generally joined together in other chain operations that are just as bad. A few independents are still left, bless 'em. It almost makes you want to salute when you pass these rugged holdouts as you go down the street to buy your groceries at the fat-cat chain. Buy your own groceries from the small grocer? Don't be ridiculous! Friendly John's a nice guy until it comes to business. Hell, he charges 50 percent more than those crooks in the chain store. John gets the business Sunday mornings or at ten at night when we've forgotten something important like a six-pack of beer. What does this whole piece of nonsense have to do with packaging waste? Plenty. The food distribution system today requires much more packaging to protect the products in the distribution pipeline. Labor costs (among others) make individual attention to either the apples or their buyers a very expensive luxury most people are not willing to pay for. Mrs. Housewife (whether liberated or not) is constantly increasing her desire for higher and higher quality products in more convenient forms. She is also willing and able to put her money (or that of her money-grubbing husband) where her mouth is and *pay* for the added services of packaging and quality control. *She* is the one to be convinced that larger sales units and decreased packaging is worth the effort in terms of decreased disposal problems. Larger purchases also require a place for storing the stuff, and that costs too.

Of course, there are technical limits to reducing material throughput by changing production processes and increasing recycling while maintaining given levels of consumption. However, substantial changes in these processes can doubtless be made with current technology and economics. Such changes would drastically alter the nature of waste materials and the harm done to the natural environment by these materials. For example, the quantity of annoying particulates (little hunks of solid crud in the smoke) belched into the atmosphere from coal-burning electrical generating plants can vary from about 20 pounds per ton of coal burned to 240 pounds per ton of coal burned. The maximum is twelve times the level of the minimum. The differences are accounted for by variations in the operating levels of the plants, the type of boiler in which the coal is burned, and the quality of the coal itself (low-sulfur-content coal is becoming increasingly expensive). Basically, these factors affect the completeness of the combustion prodess, which in turn determines the type and quantity of waste products. The more efficient plants *still* generate plenty of by-products from the combustion process, but these consist of virtually harmless water vapor and carbon dioxide.

Paper plants have been able to convert many of their manu-facturing processes to the sulfate process instead of the older sulfite process. In doing so, they have been able to reduce as much as 90 to 95 percent of previous levels the waste loads placed on watercourses. The primary difference is due to in-creased recycling of by-products that previously were dis-charged as waste. Now these components are part of the economically valuable end product. The end product, paper, will still ultimately end up in the natural environment, but increasing the number of uses or reuses between the time the resources leave the natural environment and the time they return clearly reduces the waste loadings.

Even if the natural environment was viewed as being *infinitely* valuable in its untouched state, it still wouldn't make much sense to use all the means available to reduce waste. The natural environment does possess the ability to receive, assimilate, and convert some levels of waste with no measur-able impact on itself. In other words, none of the characteristics of nature that *any* man regards as valuable will be changed by *some* waste loadings of *some* types.

One of the authors of this book owns a racing sailboat with

Spartan cruising accommodations for two or three people. Before 1970, a good old-fashioned bucket served as a crapper (the name comes from Sir Thomas Crapper, inventor of the flush toilet, England, circa 18??) and a pissoir (the name comes from France, where these delightful little structures dot the sidewalks and make it possible to relieve internal pressures while tipping your hat to passing friends and neighbors). Now, do you seriously think that my biological wastes plus those of my crew could significantly alter the ecology of Lake Michigan? Good grief, I hope not! Clearly, the problem arises when these picturesque little boats start getting so thick that you could walk on them from shore to shore without getting wet. Add to this quantity problem the wastes produced by lake freighters, ocean freighters, and railroad car ferries. Even these are not enough to really spoil the lake's ecology or aesthetics. But add still further the dumpings of municipalities, industries, and households along the lake shore and the banks of the tributary rivers. Now, the old lake has *big* problems. It's not because she can't handle some crud, but rather she can't handle the loads currently dumped.

We can even throw in some numbers from the experts to confound and amaze you at this point. Concentrations of particulates in the atmosphere must exceed 70 or 80 micrograms per cubic meter per day before even the most susceptible parts of the population will suffer any sort of health effects. Water with a total dissolved solid content in excess of 1000 parts per million can still be used for irrigation of all types of plants, provided drainage is good and sufficient water is applied to promote leaching. As many as 70,000 disease-bearing flies can be produced in a cubic foot of garbage, but if this garbage is properly buried under one foot of compacted earth, no flies will emerge and the natural environment will not be changed significantly. Most dissolved solids in water can occur in concentrations of 500–600 parts per million (by volume) and still have no ill effects on man when the water is used for drinking. The water may look like the devil and be unpleasant to swim in, but it's still potable. However, a concentration of phenol compounds of less than one part per *billion* (by volume) will cause drinking water to have an objectionable taste and smell. It will appear crystal clear, but keep it away from your nose and mouth.

Now let's look in more detail at the factors that will influence the damages suffered by nature, given some specific loading of waste material, namely:

1. The environment's assimilative capacity.
2. The attributes of the waste material itself.
3. The location of the dumping with respect to human populations.

If all waste-producing activities of persons were spread uniformly over a featureless plain such that no one person's waste affected another's environment, there would be no environmental quality problem. It is only when heavy *concentrations* of populations with their production and consumption activities appear that the environment's assimilative capacities begin to be taxed. How do these assimilative capacities operate? Take particulates and sulfurous by-products released into the atmosphere. Oxidation, assisted by solar radiation, begins transformation processes. Dilution takes place as larger and larger air masses are mixed. Finally, removal from the atmosphere occurs by gravity, rainfall, and impaction, so the junk returns to the earth and waters from whence it came. Organic wastes are acted upon by life forms present in every watercourse and reduced to harmless constituent chemicals in the process. Some inorganic waste materials, such as chlorides, are not readily broken down in the watercourses but are transported and spread through such large volumes of water that amounts of the pollutant become insignificantly small. No noticeable or *subtle* impairment of the environment occurs until the absolute volume of waste materials *exceeds zero by a substantial amount.*

It is obvious that assimilative capacities fluctuate widely on the basis of both natural and man-made factors. Winds blow at varying speeds, and different amounts of water are found in water courses during different seasons. The atmosphere of the Los Angeles basin has a lower waste-assimilative capacity in the summer months because of lower wind speeds, higher temperatures, and more intense sunlight than in other seasons. Many streams that are roaring torrents in the spring and early summer months become trickles or dry beds in the hottest months. A south wind in Milwaukee covers the McKinley marina with the stench of the human fertilizer plant referred to earlier. A west wind blows the innocent-looking white vapor out over Lake Michigan, where it bothers no one but an occasional crazy sailor. By the time the stench gets across the lake, it isn't stench anymore. Dilution has done the trick.

Regular variations in assimilative capacities even occur in the rather short period of twenty-four hours or less. For example, solar energy heats and mixes the air over many cities and therefore allows dilution of waste materials in that air to take place. But at night, the solar energy is no longer sufficient to cause this mixing and diluting. The assimilative capacity of the atmosphere is therefore reduced. The vertical depth of air available to absorb the pollutants may be reduced by as much as 98 percent compared to the daytime situation.

The factor of time has another potential impact on the assimilative capacities of the environment. For some types of waste materials, the simultaneous discharge of two or more different wastes uses up the capacities *faster* than would be the case were the discharges made separately or in different time intervals. This phenomenon, known as *synergism,* means simply that the total effect of two wastes combining together is greater than the sum of their separate impacts. The National Academy of Sciences cites an Illinois case in which waste materials made up of plaster and gypsum came in contact with chlorine-treated water. By themselves, the chlorinated water and the gypsum products were harmless, but when combined, hydrogen sulfide (like rotten eggs) was generated. This gas entered the local atmosphere and proceeded to blacken paint on forty-six houses and to stink up the place in an unbelievable manner. A better known example is the famous Los Angeles smog. In order to get the full impact of this delightful phenomenon, just the right proportions of hydrocarbons, nitrogen oxides, sunlight, and humidity must be present. Another example is the interaction of sulfur dioxide and nitric oxide, both of which are pollutants in their own rights. However, put them together and you have an even deadlier pollutant—sulfuric acid.

The previous discussions should have suggested another possible way in which the environmental quality problem might be alleviated, at least in some instances. Nature *does* have limited assimilative capacities. The capacity *may be increased* by changing the timing of disposal flows or the location of the flows themselves. Any of these courses of action require investment. By this we mean that resources which have alternative uses of value to man must be expended to carry out the augmentation of nature's assimilative capacities. The implication of this investment requirement will be discussed in more detail in the following chapters. Here we are discussing *technically* feasible aspects of the problem. The discussion of the economics will (and must) come soon enough.

Sometimes this augmentation is a side effect of other projects. For example, the planting of trees in a watershed reduces soil erosion and therefore the suspended solids and dissolved solids in the watercourse. This reduction makes it possible for man to dump more of his own wastes into the water without exceeding its assimilative capacity.

The most widely acknowledged means of augmenting capacity is building structures of one kind or another. In air pollution, this alternative has limited application except for equipment that merely exchanges air pollution for water or solid waste pollution. About the only way in which the capacity of an air resource can be increased is to build higher smokestacks from which to discharge wastes. These higher stacks permit use of air layers previously unused and can relieve the loadings in the lower levels. The rather startling proposal has been made that giant fans should be set up to blow the smog from the Los Angeles basin into the desert. If it were technically and economically feasible to implement the suggestion, such fans would augment the air resource's capacity to handle waste.

The possibilities of augmenting assimilative capacities of water and land resources are much greater. Dams can be built which store water in surplus periods and release it in low-flow periods. Storage basins exist all over the country whose purpose is to store liquid waste until the flow of water in the nearest watercourse is sufficient to remove it. Canals and pipelines exist to move water from basins where it is plentiful to basins where it is scarce.

It is in solid waste disposal, however, that the augmenting of assimilative capacities is most prevalent. At the very least, some investment is required in transportation to move solid wastes. New York City maintains a fleet of barges to dump its garbage thirty miles at sea. Milwaukee is considering the use of railroad trains to haul its junk to the Wisconsin countryside. (Anyone who has ever lived in a small community remembers his trips to the local dump.) After investment in transportation equipment, substantial outlays are often used for compacting solid wastes, thus increasing the amounts that can be placed in a given area. This compacting equipment ranges from the bulldozers used in dumps and sanitary landfills to automobile presses. Finally, since solid wastes take up scarce space, an outlay must generally be made in order to obtain a disposal site. All these actions help alleviate the problem; without them, urban dwellers would soon be buried under their own crud. Look at the mess when New York's garbage men went on strike. The city's own limited space was soon choked with the remains of consumption and production activities.

We have seen that the environment has assimilative capacities even in its natural state. We have also had examples of how this capacity can be augmented by various forms of investment. We have not as yet talked about *economizing* on the limited capacities that are available, whether natural or augmented. The discharge of wastes per se does not create pollution. *Pollution occurs when subsequent uses of natural resources are affected by waste discharges.* Waste producers differ in the types of wastes they discharge, their location when discharging wastes, and the times they release the waste products. It might be nice, but right now it just isn't feasible to locate a coal-burning electric generating plant in the middle of the Atlantic Ocean.

Similarly, those who suffer from deterioration of the natural environment differ drastically in the types of damage they suffer, when they suffer the damages, and what measures they can take to alleviate the problem. A seventy-year old emphysema sufferer who has been a lifetime four-pack-a-day man is much more irritated by an atmosphere loaded with junk than is the robust jogger who daily trots three miles to the office.

The implications of the above paragraph should not be overlooked! It is *possible* to rearrange in time and space the locations of waste producers and waste sufferers *such that the damages suffered are minimized.* Assume, for example, that the atmosphere is the only place available for disposal of wastes. Were this the case, it would make sense to place all waste-producing activities downwind and all sufferers upwind. As long as you had enough room upwind for everyone, no problem. But if you ran out of room, the most susceptible sufferers would be placed farthest upwind to the waste-generating plant and the least susceptible closest to it. The distances sufferers would locate away from the generating plant would vary inversely with sufferer susceptibility and/or ability (including ability from varying incomes) to adjust to the pollution. The emphysema victim would be located all the way upwind. Because of his respiratory condition, he is extremely sensitive to air pollution and few if any measures other than avoidance will alleviate the problem. On the other hand, the jogger's respiratory system is capable of handling fairly severe stresses with little ill effect. His automobile may get awfully dirty in this location, but the cost of cleaning it is small. In fact, if he's a real health nut, he may not even have an automobile.

In the story *The Secret of Santa Vittoria,* a small Italian town is described in which a stream is used both for water and for waste disposal. Each family dips drinking water from the stream as it passes the family's door, and dumps its waste in the same place at which the drinking water is taken. As you might guess, the fat cats lived upstream and the poorest slobs lived the farthest downstream. Each inhabitant's relative wealth and income could be accurately estimated by his upstream or downstream location. Closer to home, the wealthy in virtually every American city and town live upwind from locations where heavy air pollution is produced.

Obviously, the world is not organized in the neat manner described above. Time and space considerations are *not* based solely on pollution creation and avoidance. The reason is because to do so would involve costs *greater than* the people concerned are prepared to pay. If electricity for Denver had to be generated in the middle of the Atlantic Ocean, it's probable that Denver wouldn't have a heck of a lot of power. Even if it were technically feasible to perform this feat, the cost of such a program would be enormous.

A similar problem of choice exists for the man with emphysema. He might live an extra year or two by moving from New York City to the mountains of Alberta or Wyoming. If he leaves New York, he must give up all the booze and broads associated with the city. He may very well feel that two extra years just ain't worth the sacrifice. Of course, he can take a compromise position and stay in air-conditioned buildings in New York when the pollution is particularly bad. This last course of action points up another possibility in handling pollution. Not all adjustments to pollution must come from the producers of the crud. Just as the waste generator may change his production processes to generate a smaller volume of waste, so too can the sufferer modify his behavior to minimize damages. Rather than stay in his apartment, the emphysema sufferer may buy a gas mask or may move to the mountains. More realistically, the water consumed by some communities in this country is nothing more than reconstituted sewage water from somewhere else. Reconstituted, it is still a perfectly good product. Some buildings in cities are now being surfaced with material which, when attacked by chemicals in the atmosphere, peels off in thin layers to expose another yet untarnished surface. In fact, it is unusual when the sufferer of pollution cannot take *some* action that will at least reduce the damages he suffers. Be careful now! We haven't suggested what anyone *should* do at any point in this chapter. We're discussing all *feasible* courses of action, not just "fair" ones.

Scattered throughout the preceding pages is the notion that man has four general courses of action open to him with respect to his use of the natural environment's assimilative capacities.

1. He can make his many decisions in life without regard to any of the limitations of these assimilative capacities.

Clearly, he does not follow this extreme course. Otherwise, steel mills would be located in fine residential areas and houses wouldn't have toilets.

2. He can augment this assimilative capacity. This alternative involves investment of scarce resources to modify the time flow of capacity or to make new portions of the environment available for waste disposal.

3. Another alternative is to modify waste-generating activities so that they are better coordinated with the assimilative capacities, natural or augmented. Recovery and reuse of waste material, modification of product output, and changes in production processes all fall into this category.

4. Finally, the sufferer can modify his behavior and activities so that pollution's impact on him is reduced.

Each of the above alternatives and its several versions are simply representations of more basic properties which all adjustment processes must possess. Whether talking about the construction of dams, the waste materials of paper mills, or the air inhaled by emphysema sufferers, our concern has consistently been the adjustment to some *volume* measure of waste materials. Reductions in environmental quality have been synonymous with increases in the absolute *volume* of crud being dumped into the environment. Conversely, increases in this quality have been synonymous with reductions in the absolute *volume* of the crud.

At first glance, the concept of volume seems simple and adequate. It refers to nothing more than the total amount of something or other. However, a bit of thought shows it to be a rather empty concept *unless it can be related to the idea of time.* The usual way of putting this together is to talk in terms of *rates,* that is, the amount of waste materials dumped per time unit. This particular notion is the one we will be using throughout much of this book. But even this relation is not always adequate to express the volume–time importance. In particular, it does not take into account the importance of the *interval* over which a rate of discharge takes place. It also does not recognize the importance of the point in time at which the dumping may start.

The importance of the interval of time over which a given rate of discharge is expected to occur is shown by the following example. Suppose we are interested in determining the damage function which relates breathing sulfur dioxide and the health of the human lung. After looking at the literature, we find two sources which appear to have the information we want.

One source indicates that a man can ingest a very high volume of SO_2 over a short period—say one thousand units over ten hours—and not be adversely affected. The second study indicates that a man ingesting very small quantities of SO_2 over a long time interval—say ten units over one thousand hours—will be seriously damaged. To find the rate in each case, we merely divide the total volume by the number of hours. If we then "analyze" the rates and results in the two studies, we find that people ingesting high rates of SO_2 suffer less damage than people ingesting low rates of SO_2. I guess we'd better recommend that everyone go out and breathe all the rotten eggs he can find!

Naturally, when faced with the preceding foolishness, one realizes something has been left out of the analysis. That something is the *time interval over which the ingestion takes place*. However, even when this aspect is brought into the analysis, one temporal factor is still ignored. The question of *when* the SO_2 ingestion is started can make a big difference in the effect of the ingestion.

Assume for the moment that the rate of SO_2 ingestion and length of the period over which ingestion will take place are fixed; that is, whatever you do, you can't change these two factors. However, assume you do have a choice of starting the ingestion now or waiting twenty-five years to begin the process. Whichever time you choose to begin, your lungs will start in the same condition, and in either case the duration and rate of ingestion will kill you. The choice you're going to make is obvious unless you prefer dying now. As a general principle, man prefers that things he doesn't like be shoved as far in the future as possible. Similarly, he prefers that enjoyable things be brought as close to the present as possible.

We have seen that recycling of materials reduces the total throughput needed to maintain a given level of economic activity. We have also made the point that all materials must return to the natural environment sooner or later as waste products. Recycling, therefore, has the additional advantage of postponing an undesirable happening (waste in the natural environment) as well as reducing throughput resources.

It should now be apparent that temporal factors are most important in considering the pollution problem. The sufferer might change the damages he has suffered by reducing the *rate* of exposure to the pollutant. He might also try to reduce the exposure period or push the period farther into the future. No other possibilities exist, assuming the sufferer cannot control output levels of the crud. Waste generators try to change their production processes, to take pollution control measures, or to change output to adjust the way they produce crud in terms of these three temporal factors. Again, there are no other ways. All environmental quality problems fundamentally involve adjustments in the rate, time interval, or initiation time of waste discharges, assimilative capacities, or sufferer exposure.

3
CHAPTER

The Theory
of Crud—
Without Heresy

So far, we've ranged the field in discussing certain philosophies and technologies that impinge on the problem of environmental quality. Now it's time to get to the heart of some aspects of the matter with which your authors are supposed to have some expertise. We aren't going to assume very much knowledge of economic theory on your part, but we are going to expose you to some analytical tools. As we said in Chapter 1, don't get uptight just because you see a few graphs and a couple of simple formulas! You all have headpieces. For those of you who have had a standard economics principles course, Chapter 3 is mostly review. Chapter 4 will introduce some current heresy into the theoretical constructs of this chapter, so the review will probably be good for you anyway. Constantly keep in mind that these analytical tools are just that—*tools*. Without a good sharp saw, the best carpenter in the world has a devil of a time cutting a two-by-four. By the same token, even a home hacker can do a passible job of cutting, given a good saw and a little knowledge of its use. Of course, the hacker can also lop off a few fingers if he *mis*uses the tool. Think about it.

We'll begin by classifying our material world into some convenient segments (see Figure 3.1). These are not rigid classifications but merely groupings which lay the groundwork for the analysis that follows. Our world consists of "things." We're not going to argue with the philosophers and/or theologians who might maintain that things exist only when there's a man or men around to acknowledge their existence. We will assert that the things of this world either affect men's lives or don't affect men's lives—they either yield *services* to men or yield *disservices* to men. The rock on top of a mountain in the Rockies doesn't mean much to man until it is seen and enjoyed as scenery *by man* (it is yielding a service) or until it rolls down the mountain and clobbers a car passing on the valley highway (almost certainly a disservice to someone). For our purposes, then, the rock is considered a *nongood* as long as it *yields no service or no disservice,* and it is a *good* if it *yields services or disservices.*

The other categories into which we must subdivide goods is based on the scarcity or abundance of the item in conjunction with its beneficial or harmful impact on man. If looking at the rock on the mountain means that something has to be given up, then the service yielded by the rock (part of the beautiful view) is *not free.* The service of the rock is now *economic* in that something else has to be forgone in order to obtain it. Similarly, if the rock will stay put without expending resources to hold it on top of the heap, no problem. However, if a retaining wall must be built to keep it from clobbering automobiles, the potential *disservice* of the rock is again *economic.* Therefore, it is useful to differentiate goods into those which *cost* something to *get* or *get rid of* and those which are *free*—nothing need be given up to have or have not. Remember, we have also said that the degree of scarcity or abundance has something to do with this cost element. Someone who can often see as beautiful a view as our rock on the mountain will probably be less willing to pay to look at our particular rock than he would be if our view were unique. Motorists and the State Highway Department might not be willing to spend much to retain a pebble on the mountain top. If there is a whole mess of pebbles or if the pebble is a boulder, the willingness to expend resources will

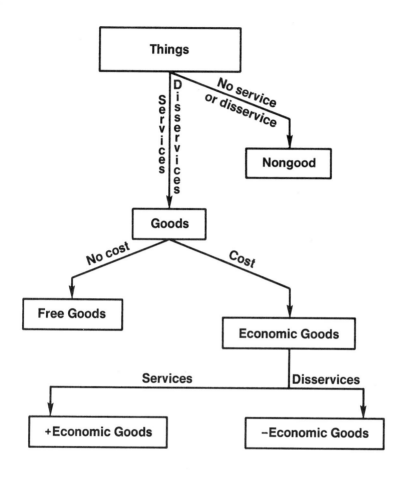

Figure 3.1   The Material World

increase considerably. The single pebble may scratch the finish of your chariot, but the boulder may smash the hell out of it.

We have already mentioned the final categorization made among economic goods. If the good yields a service, it is a *positive good*. If the good yields a disservice, it is a *negative good*.

Having described some of the meat of our broad subject

matter, let's push forward with some very basic economic analysis. How do people improve their lot on this earth? Again, philosophers and others have a field day just arguing what constitutes an improved lot before even getting to the question of how to improve it. We'll bypass some of the niceties of that discussion and just assume for now that increased goods and services are *one* of the elements of an improved lot. Perhaps this isn't true for the Jackies and Aris of this world; but for most of us slobs, having more goodies available at least increases the range of choice facing us. This choice may include giving up more goods in preference for a simple life. Fair enough! The choice, however, doesn't even exist unless the goods are there to begin with.

In the beginning, there was man, and man spent all his time (the only resource he possessed) doing his *things* to keep body and soul together. Notice, we said doing his *things,* not *thing.* He had only his time and brute strength with which to work. His economic choices consisted only of how to allocate these between productive work of several different types and (yes, even then) leisure. Soon he learned the joys of procrastination, and his choices expanded to do it now or do it tomorrow. Then he learned how to make tools of one form or another which made his productive activities more productive. Here again, he had to choose between working to make productive tools and giving up consumption activities *now* or to keep on doing his things the same old tried, true, and inefficient ways. Somewhere along the line, man number one met man number two and after initially scaring each other out of their loincloths, they began to compare notes. George found out that Clinton was a helluva lot better at clobbering meat-type animals, and similarly Clinton found out that George was a real fireball when it came to catching and skinning clothing-type animals. Since both used both products, they hit on a masterful idea. Each would do that job for which he had the greatest talent. Clinton gets the meat and George gets the skins. Of course, if this happens, the total product in the two-man society goes up. But the increased production is *useful* only if the extra skins George produces can be *traded* for the extra meat Clinton produces. A multiperson exchange economy essentially similar to today's was then born.

1. If a man is to increase his material well-being above a subsistence level, he must specialize.
2. If a man specializes in producing one good, he must *trade* to obtain the other goods he wants.

Men have developed preferences (different preferences for different men). Along with these preferences, they have endowments of resources and finished goods and services at any moment in time. Two ways are available to improve their well-being, given preferences and endowments. First of all, they can *transform* one resource or good into something else that either *they* like better or *their neighbor* likes better. Second, they can *exchange* some part of their endowment or production for another combination of goods and services they like better. This seems like a simple enough set of concepts, but brothers and sisters, the implications of these simple principles can and do fill volumes.

Why do people want what they want? Don't ask the economist. It just ain't his bag. Better you should go to the headshrinker. How do people express their wants? Now we're back in an area we can talk about. One answer to this question is found in the political arenas of the world. In this country, you can write your congressman or vote the bum out of office if he doesn't have a "good" batting average. Of course, "good" means *you* think it's good. Someone else might not agree and the bum might stay in office. A second and related way in which preferences are expressed is through force. Maybe this takes the form of revolution or just a simple clot on the jaw of that stupid knothead who doesn't share your preferences. Force has always been used by man in settling some issues of scarcity. It continues to be used now and then, primarily because it seems to work. If you don't like some guy or his ideas or his claims to some property or other, *kill him.* He may have the same brainstorm, however, and everybody ends up dead (but not red?).

Fortunately, there is another way to allocate **scarce goods**. It is used today in virtually all countries and economies to a greater or lesser extent. It is called the *market*. You all know what a market is in one form or another. In its most general form, it involves some type of interaction between people that are buying something and people that are selling something. These people get together either personally or by telephone or through brokers or a department store, and after a greater or lesser amount of bargaining arrive at a price at which the seller is *willing* and *able* to sell and the buyer is *willing* and *able* to buy. The price—that which buyers are willing and able to part with and which sellers are willing and able to accept—will bring the quantities offered and demanded into equilibrium. This merely means the quantity offered (supplied) will equal the quantity demanded. It can be shown (and you can thank your lucky stars we're not going to show it here) that this solution is optimal in that once it is obtained, nobody—neither buyer or seller—can be made any better off without making some-one else worse off. Of course, the assumption underlying this optimal solution is that individual free choice is a desirable characteristic in the economy. This point is often neglected or forgotten, but it is very important. There are some other as-sumptions, which we will discuss in a moment, but for now, let us illustrate a market operation and see just what's involved. Since we're supposed to be discussing environmental quality, we'll take as our example a widely used air pollution control device—body deodorant.

In Figure 3.2, we show a graph of the prices demanders of deodorant are willing and able to pay, in conjunction with the several quantities they are willing and able to take at these prices. The sweat is probably pouring out from many of your brows, but relax! That graph is easy to read and will save a lot of very dull reading if you'll only get used to using it. Clearly, the quantity of deodorant people are going to demand is going to depend on several other factors besides the price of the stuff. To name a few, the quantity demanded will depend upon the price of the deodorant (as we have just said), the price of goods related to the deodorant, the incomes of the demanders, the tastes of the demanders, and the transaction costs facing the buyers when using the market. At any one time, then, quantity demanded will depend on all these things. Therefore, if we graph the relation between just *price* and *quantity demanded,* we will have to mentally or analytically "hold constant" all the other factors. If any of the other factors change, we will have to reconstruct a new relation between price and quantity demanded. In other words, if any factor *other than* the price of the product changes, the *demand curve* (that's what we call the relation between just price and quantity demanded) will *shift* its position on the graph.

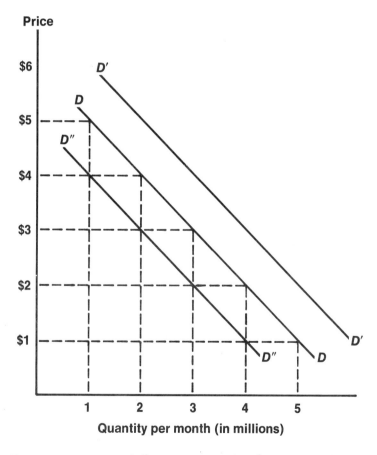

Figure 3.2 Demand for Spray Deodorant (12-ounce cans)

Before going any further, let's get some simple shorthand that will reduce the cases of writer's cramp and save a great deal of time.

We're going to assign symbols to each variable mentioned. Thus:

Price of the good $= p$
Price of related goods $= p_r$
Income $= i$
Tastes $= t$
Transactions costs $= ICP_d$
Quantity demanded $= q_d$

There's nothing tough about that, right? The next step is to use some notation many of you learned in high school. It is called an implicit function, but don't let that shake you. Instead of saying that the quantity demanded of a good depends upon . . ., we could also say that the quantity of a good *is a function* of . . . . In notational form, this translates into

$$q_d = f(. . .)$$

There's the skeleton. Now all that remains is to fill in the blanks between the parentheses with the variables we're interested in. Each of these variables is separated by a comma.

$$q_d = f(p, P_r, i, t, ICP_d)$$

This little combination of symbols says exactly the same thing as all the words that preceded it.

Two other bits of notation are desirable at this point. If one wishes to hold some of the variables constant, he can do so by placing a bar over the top of the variable symbol, as, for example, $\bar{p}_r$. The symbolic expression of the demand function is thus:

$$q_d = f(p, \bar{p}_r, \bar{i}, \bar{t}, \overline{ICP}_d)$$

Quantity changes with changing prices, *everything else being held constant*. We obtain the quantities that people are willing and able to buy at different prices when all other factors are kept the same.

Finally, we indicate increases or decreases in a variable
with an arrow going either up $(\overset{\uparrow}{p_r})$ or down $(\underset{\downarrow}{p_r})$. Notice that our *implicit function* doesn't yet pretend to tell us *how* quantity demanded is related to the several variables. All it says so far is that relation exists. *How* they are related is covered in the following paragraphs. Now that you're all mathematicians, we'll stride boldly forward.

To actually derive a demand curve is a bloody difficult business, to say the least. For our purposes, however, we'll assume that we send out to all potential buyers of spray deodorant in 12-ounce cans a questionnaire which gives them a series of prices in dollars and cents. We ask them to prepare this questionnaire at exactly 12:01 tomorrow afternoon and tell us what quantities of this deodorant they would be willing and able to purchase at various price alternatives. We aren't asking them what quantities they *are* going to purchase tomorrow afternoon, but rather their willingness and ability to buy this product should they face different price alternatives. This is *not* the way we would actually gain information to construct a statistical demand curve, since answers to a hypothetical, what-would-you-do-if question are not very useful. The actual methods of getting this information are complex and are not discussed here. After analyzing our returned questionnaires, we find that at lower alternative prices more and more people would be willing and able to buy more and more of the product. At $5 per can, one million cans would have been sold; at $1 per can, five million cans would have been sold with all the conditions *as they existed at 12:01 that day.* In other words, by making a "photoflash picture" at an instant in time, we effectively hold constant all the other factors affecting quantity demanded.

If all factors affecting quantity demanded are held constant except price, our downward-sloping demand curve will result. In other words, at cheaper prices people will buy more; at more expensive prices people will buy less. This result is so general that we even call it the *law of demand.* Such statistical evidence as has been accumulated indicates that the law is correct. Even without such evidence, the bloody concept just plain makes sense. Even Richard Burton's multimillion-dollar diamond would probably fit the law. True, if the rock had been priced at $100 instead of many zeros more, Richard probably wouldn't have been interested in buying it. Its prestige value would have been very low. However, with a given prestige value for the rock, I'm sure even Richard would have been happier to pay a lower price than the higher price he paid. Again, we're using price in the most general sense of that which must be given up per unit of that which is acquired. It might have been money or even the love of Liz in this case. Again and again and again, *remember*! This price–quantity relation assumes that all other factors affecting quantity demanded are being held constant. Now let's look at the impact of these other factors.

Related goods can be of two types—substitutes and complements. Substitutes are things which will do just about the same thing as the given good, at least in some uses. Certainly, two 6-ounce cans would be a substitute for one 12-ounce can in most circumstances. Bath soap is a partial substitute for deodorant. Even air conditioners could be substituted for at least a measure of deodorant use. As the price of a substitute goes up, the demand curve for the given good will go up. If the price of bath soap goes up, we'll tend to take fewer baths and use more deodorant. This will raise the demand for deodorant, as shown in Figure 3.2. At any given price, people will be willing and able to buy more; or for any given quantity, people will be willing and able to pay a higher price.

Assume that people have a tendency to brush their teeth every time they use deodorant. This could mean that toothpaste and deodorant are complements to some extent. The use of one product implies the use of at least some of the other. If the *price* of toothpaste were to rise, the total *cost* of the clean-up process would go up and therefore the *demand* for deodorant would fall. This example may seem a bit farfetched, but some other product pairs exhibit this phenomenon very strongly. If the price of new cars increases, one can expect the *demand* for tires to decrease as a result. The quantity of cars demanded decreases *and* the demand for tires decreases. When the *price* of a particular good rises, the *demand* for its complement will fall. The converse is also true.

Income changes also affect the relation between prices and

quantities demanded. At first blush, one might think that increases in income would automatically increase the demand for a product: that is, increase the quantity demanded at any given price and/or increase the price people are willing and able to pay for any given quantity. For some goods, this is true. As a matter of fact, goods for which it is the case are called *normal* or *superior* goods. The demands for some other goods don't act this way. Take, for example, that miserable store-bought fluff laughingly called bread. What do you think happens to the demand for this junk when incomes increase? You can be assured demand falls. As incomes increase, it is possible to buy many goods that previously couldn't be afforded. These goods are purchased instead of the cheaper ones. Thus, all-butter bread is purchased instead of the all-air bread. Substitution takes place, but the substitution happens because of the increased incomes. Referring back to our deodorant demand, there is every reason to believe that deodorant is a normal or superior good. If this be the case, then as incomes of the demanders increase, the *demand* for the product will increase $(D'D')$. Should deodorant be an *inferior* good, the converse would be true and demand would fall, as in $D''D''$ in the figure.

Like most other disciplines, economics has its fudge factors, too. In demand analysis, this fudge factor takes the name of *tastes.* All kinds of psychological factors go into people's desires for goods and services. If it is possible to isolate and identify the effect of price itself, prices of related goods, income, and transaction costs, there will still be a large residual of "unexplained" purchases. We will lump these all together in the catchall taste. Obviously, if people's tastes change in favor of a given good, the demand will increase for that good $(D'D'$ in Figure 3.2). Similarly, should tastes decrease, demand will decrease $(D''D''$ in the figure). Time was, for example, that a good case of BO wasn't viewed as such a social disaster as it is today. The demand for freedom from the pollutant has increased as a result of changes in tastes, and this has changed peoples' tastes in favor of the antipollution device—deodorant.

Our final category of demand determinants is of particular importance in analyzing the economic problem of environmental quality. The category is *transactions costs,* which we will break down into three specific kinds—information costs, contractual costs, and policing costs. In fact, even the notation reflects this breakdown, and we are going to call transaction costs *ICP* costs. *ICP* costs face demanders and, as we shall see shortly, suppliers as well. Therefore, in our notation to differentiate demanders' transactions costs (ICP_d) from suppliers transactions costs (ICP_s), we use subscripts.

Many people, including economists, become so enamored of the beauty and efficiency of the market system that they tend to forget that markets themselves *cost.* Markets are not free goods, because people have to give up resources in order for markets to operate. In terms of our simple example, a great deal of money (and thus resources) is spent by deodorant manufacturers in giving "information" about their products to potential consumers, and consumers spend resources acquiring information about the availability of goods and the services these goods can offer. Right now, nothing can be gained by discussing if this "information" is worthwhile for potential customers of the economy. The point is that commercials cost, and part of that cost will be paid for by the manufacturer and part by the customer, whether he wants the information or not. One cost that TV commercials impose on TV viewers is the *time* viewers must spend watching the damn things if they wish to view the program. Assuming some alternative use for the time either in leisure or in remunerative work, this cost can be substantial. Contractual costs? Every time anyone makes a purchase of any kind, a contract is made which transfers some right or rights to the good from seller to buyer. The costs may be nothing more than the time spent by the purchaser and the wages of the check-out girl at the supermarket counter. It may also be something as major as a lawyer's fee in settling some large property right issue. Since marketing implies transfer of rights, then for these rights to have value they must be able to be enforced. An unenforced or unenforceable right *no longer is a right.* It is therefore a prerequisite for market operation that the rights transferred by the market be enforced, and this implies expenditures of resources for *policing costs.* We'll be discussing the implications of *ICP* many times throughout the rest of the book, but for now, suffice to say that increased *ICP* will decrease the demand for a good, while decreased *ICP* costs will tend to increase demand.

Now we've talked about half the market operation, but unfortunately all that we have arrived at is a *series* of prices and quantities. As yet, we do not have sufficient information to talk about *a* price and *a* quantity. For this, we need the other half of the market operation—supply. The discussion of supply is very similar to that of demand, and we won't have to spend quite so much time on it. Basically, the quantity of any particular good or service that people are willing and able to supply (q_s) will depend upon the price they can receive for the good (p), the *structure of* costs facing them in producing the good (C), the technology available with which inputs can be turned into the product in question (T), and the *ICP* costs facing suppliers. Notice that all the variables affecting quantity supplied are really special types of *costs.* Even the price of the good itself is a cost to the supplier, since it represents one possible return from the resources he controls. It is an *alternative* or *opportunity cost,* whether or not he accepts the price. While we show technology as a separate argument, this too merely influences the structure of costs facing the supplier. ICP_s costs are kept as a separate argument just so that we can conveniently look at their impact later on. The point, dear readers, is that no matter what we're talking about, the *supply* of something is going to depend on the *costs* of providing it, one way or another. Using our simpler notation, then,

$$q_s = f(p, C, T, ICP_s)$$

Notice that the only similar argument in the supply function and the demand function is the *price of the good.* All the other arguments are *dissimilar.* This follows from one of the basic assumptions generally made in standard market analysis—that *supply* and *demand* are independent. In other words, anything tending to change supply will not change demand, and vice versa. The only variable shared by both the supply and demand functions is *price,* and this little jewel is the baby that can solve the whole problem of choice through the market.

We will make one further assumption about the way in

which *price* and *quantity supplied* vary, everything else being held constant; that is, as price goes *up,* the quantity people are willing and able to produce will also go up. In other words, in general there is a *direct* relation between the price of a good and the quantity supplied. Notice, this is just the opposite of the case with demand. The quantity of a good demanded goes *down* as price goes up. In Figure 3.3, we graph the *supply* of 12-ounce cans of spray deodorant—supply meaning quantity supplied at different prices, everything else held constant. This graph reflects our assumption that as price increases, the

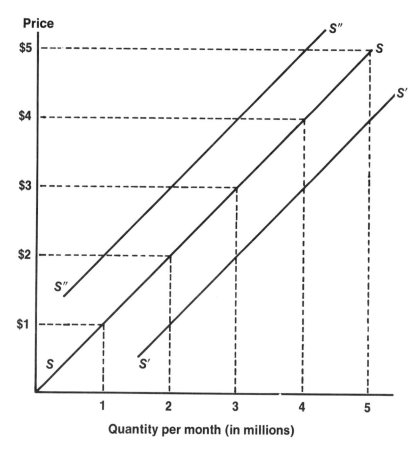

Figure 3.3 Supply of Spray Deodorant (12-ounce cans)

quantity people are willing and able to supply also increases. Really, this makes sense for almost all goods and services. At this level of analysis, we'll just ask you to agree that while exceptions can (and do) exist, this assumption makes sense for most cases. Most producers of anything have alternatives to which their productive resources can be directed. It is reasonable that with a higher price for some particular product, more resources will be drawn into the production of that product and output will increase (given that all other prices appear to remain the same). From this, we obtain the direct relation between prices and quantities and our upward-sloping supply curve.

The other arguments affecting quantity supplied operate in a fairly obvious way. As *costs* facing the supplier increase, the quantity he is willing and able to produce will decrease *at any given price*. Hence, supply will be decreased, that is, shifted to the left (S"S" in Figure 3.3). The converse is true for decreases in the cost structure facing suppliers. Such a decrease will tend to increase the quantity they are willing and able to produce at any given price—a downward to-the-right shift of the supply curve, as illustrated by S'S' in Figure 3.3.

An improvement in the technology available means that any given set of inputs, or a different combination of inputs, is more productive than before. That is, more output can be produced for a given money outlay. This phenomenon will also tend to shift the supply curve to the right—an increase in *supply*. Finally, the transactions costs facing suppliers are but one of the total costs they face. These costs could have been included in the C (cost structure) argument, but because they are going to be so important in the discussions that follow, we have abstracted them as a special category of costs—ICP_s. As with other costs, an increase in ICP_s will tend to decrease supply (S"S"), and a decrease in ICP_s will tend to increase supply (S'S').

Again, it should be emphasized that although we have placed several arguments in our supply function, *all these arguments represent costs in one form or another*. Our cost structure (C) represents the costs of our inputs. The technology variable (T) is the cost of putting these inputs together. The

ICP$_s$ concerns the cost of marketing the product, and the price itself represents our cost if we should produce an alternative product.

Okay, that's all you need in order to observe the operation of simple markets. We have developed two functions whose only common variable is *price*. In one function, quantity *increases* as price increases (supply), and in the other, quantity *decreases* as price increases (demand). Price is the jewel that can adjust the quantities supplied and demanded so that neither surpluses nor shortages exist. Does supply or demand determine price? Anyone who has ever used a pair of scissors can answer that one. Does the upper or the lower blade of the scissors cut the cloth? The answer, of course, is that neither one *alone* does the job. *Both operating together* divide the cloth for the seamstress and the goodies for a market economy.

If we assume that everyone knows all the time exactly what's going on, and if we have many independent buyers and many independent sellers, then the price and quantity at *equilibrium* will be *optimal* and *unique*. Both these conditions should be explained a bit. Going back to the deodorant market, Figure 3.4 illustrates the supply and demand functions previously developed, but now they are superimposed on each other. Notice that there is one point at which the two "curves" cross— $3 and three million cans per month. Economists usually describe this point as "optimal" because, *given free choice*, no buyer or seller can be made *better off* without making some other buyer or seller worse off. At market quantities *less than* equilibrium, demanders would be willing and able to pay *higher* prices than those required to induce suppliers to supply. Demand, which represents this willingness and ability, is greater than supply, which represents suppliers' willingness and ability. Increased production and trade will improve the positions of both groups without anyone losing. Conversely, quantities greater than equilibrium are consistent with prices which are lousy for both groups. The market facing suppliers is represented by the demand curve to the right of the equilibrium point. All these quantities greater than equilibrium mean that prices required by suppliers to produce are greater than prices demanders are willing and able to pay for the increased quantities. One or both of the groups could be better off by reducing

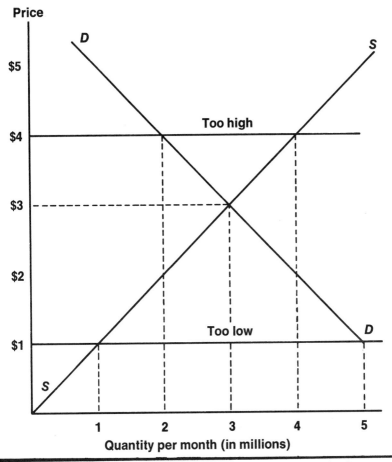

Price

$5

$4   **Too high**

$3

$2

$1   **Too low**

D   S

S   D

1   2   3   4   5

Quantity per month (in millions)

*Figure 3.4 The Market—Supply and Demand—for
Spray Deodorant (12-ounce cans)*

the market quantity back to equilibrium. Don't feel bad if this
concept doesn't jump off the paper into your skullpiece. It's not
that simple, but, boy, is it useful once you get it!

Let's consider the outcome when there exists a disequi-
librium price established by some central authority which dis-
approves of the equilibrium price arrived at by the market. For
example, if the price should be set at $4 per can (too high), the
quantity people would be willing and able to demand would fall
from three million to two million cans (the stuff is too damn
expensive, say many people), and the quantity people are will-

ing and able to supply increases from three million to four million cans (it's a good deal compared to the suppliers' alternative production choices). Clearly, we have a problem, since q_s exceeds q_d. We have an *economic surplus*. Unless somebody comes in and says you *must* buy the crud at $4, there will be just too much around, and in their desire to get rid of the stuff, suppliers will start cutting prices. As the price falls, the quantity demanded will begin to rise and the quantity supplied will begin to fall (*supply and demand have not changed*). Finally, we're back at the old equilibrium price and quantity. In the same way, should the price be too low, say $1 per can, quantity supplied would exceed quantity demanded ($q_s = 1,000,000$ and $q_d = 5,000,000$ in our example), and there would be an *economic shortage*. Now, demanders would start bidding up the price for the short item, and as price increased, the quantity demanded would begin to *decrease* and quantity supplied would begin to *increase,* thus working back to the old equilibrium price and quantity.

You've probably already figured out what will happen if one of the arguments in either the supply or demand function changes, but here are some examples anyway. In Figure 3.5a, we have taken our deodorant market as before, but now assume that supply increases. This could come about by decreasing the cost structure facing deodorant suppliers, *improving* the level of technology available to them, or decreasing the ICP_s costs facing them. An increase in supply such as that shown by $S'S'$ or for any of these changes, the market price will tend to *decrease* and the equilibrium quantity supplied and demanded will tend to increase. Conversely, a decrease in supply can be caused by increasing the cost structure facing suppliers, including an increase in ICP_s. *A decaying of the available technology* would also decrease supply. A war which destroys youth and factories could reduce the technology available to society if no one was left who knew the various production processes. This decrease is illustrated by $S''S''$ in Figure 3.5a. Notice that such a decrease will tend to raise the equilibrium level of prices and to decrease the equilibrium quantity supplied and demanded.

In a similar manner, changing the value of the arguments in the demand function will *shift* the demand curve, either

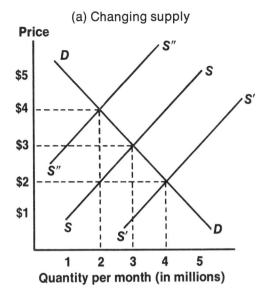

(a) Changing supply

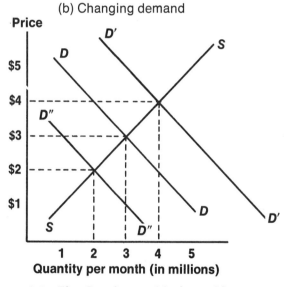

(b) Changing demand

Figure 3.5   The Deodorant Market—Changing Supply
and Demand (12-ounce cans)

increasing demand (*D'D'* in Figure 3.5b) or *decreasing* demand (*D"D"* in the figure). If deodorant is a normal or a superior good, increasing the incomes of the demanders will increase demand and raise equilibrium price and quantity. If it is an inferior good (this is unlikely), demand will decrease and both equilibrium price and quantity will be decreased. Assuming our bath soap substitute increases in *price,* the *demand* for deodorant will increase, thus increasing equilibrium price and quantity. These are virtually mechanical motions at this point, but remember that they reflect very important and precise economic actions and reactions, given the validity of our basic assumptions—implicit and explicit. The next chapter is going to examine some of these assumptions in more detail.

Now it's time to begin the economic analysis of our specific subject—environmental quality. To begin, we'll keep it simple and use examples you all will understand. Our demand for deodorant just discussed is really what the economist would call a *derived demand.* The service provided by the deodorant is the reduction of body odor. Body odor can pollute the air we live in. Therefore, the demand for deodorant is derived from the more general demand for BO-free air. The supply of deodorant conceptually amounts to a supply of "cleaner" air than would exist without the deodorant. Let's assume that you are a student in a mass lecture of English Literature 101 and that your class is held in a cramped lecture hall with insufficient ventilation. (Since it is unlikely that this book will be used by English lit professors, we're picking on them.) The second, obviously unrealistic assumption is that your prof has an absolutely monumental and continual case of BO. All you pristine students don't suffer this problem, so the only air polluter is easily identified as the prof. Assume further that the BO doesn't bother him in the slightest and he doesn't care a bit about your collective sensitivities. He's an admirer of the English nobility. Therefore, he refuses to use and pay for the control instrument (deodorant). Two basic solutions are possible in this case, both depending on who owns the air in the lecture hall.

Assume first that the no-good administration of the university decides that the prof has the right (and enforces this right) to use the air in the lecture room the way he sees fit. This is known as academic freedom. In this case, if you want to cut down the pollution, you're going to have to *pay* the prof. Look at Figure 3.6. Here we have shown the class's demand for BO-free air in the lecture room. No numbers are shown on the axes,

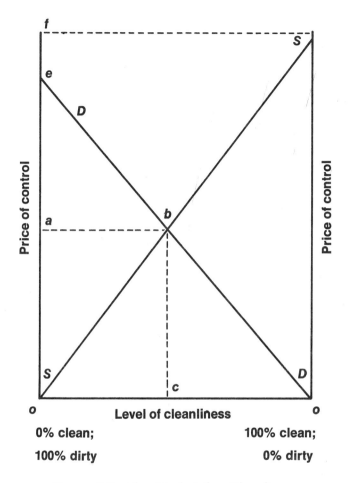

Figure 3.6   The Market for Cleanliness

because all we're showing is that as the cost (price) of clean air increases, the quantity you are willing and able to "buy" will decrease. Think about it. This is probably absolutely accurate as a prediction of your behavior. If someone says, pay the prof a penny a lecture and he'll quit polluting, you might do it. If the cost to you is $100 per lecture for the same level of purity, you'll probably put up with a helluva stench. Similarly, if the prof uses a little control (deodorant), the level of cleanliness will increase. As he uses more (hence, more cost), further increases in cleanliness will result. Our supply curve for clean air is upward sloping to the right. In describing the market, nobody has said anything about the rights to the air. All we are saying is that increased levels of cleanliness are going to bear a higher price tag, and higher price tags are going to cut down the quantity demanded of the clean air.

Now back to the assumption that the prof has the right to the air, including the right to pollute it. Figure 3.6 indicates that if zero price is paid for cleaning up the atmosphere, the old prof will implement zero control measures and we have maximum full-bore pollution (point o). Notice that for this zero level of control, "the class" will be willing and able to pay a price of oe for a beginning measure of control. The prof will be willing and able to use some deodorant for a much smaller price (beginning at o and going up the supply curve). Therefore, with perfect knowledge, certainty, and free market operations, trade will take place and students will start "buying off" the prof, that is, paying him to increase his use of deodorant. This process will continue until the price of the control is equal to the price people are willing and able to pay for that level of control. In our example, this will occur at price oa and level of cleanliness oc. The total amount spent to control the pollution will equal the price of control (oa) times the level of control (oc), or a total dollar value of resources equal to the area $oabc$. Notice several other characteristics of our market. If a zero price exists for control, the quantity demanded by the students will be od, but the control supplied by the prof at zero price is zero. Similarly, if absolute cleanliness is the goal, the prof will have to be paid a price of of.

Now let's change the rules of the game and assume that the student power movement is able to convince the administration of the errors of its ways and gains the rights to the air in Lecture Room 3-A. *That's* surely going to whip the pollution problem *right now* because that smelly prof can't use the air to discharge his effluence *without the students' permission.* Wait a minute! Has anything really changed as far as the market is concerned? Demanders still have the same feelings about the pollution, and the cost of control hasn't changed. So what's going to happen if we allow a free market with perfect knowledge, certainty, and zero transactions costs? At the point of 100 percent control (*od*), the students are not willing to pay anything to *increase* control. However, 100 percent control is costing the professor a bundle. To maintain this virgin purity (of the air), he has to practically keep immersed in deodorant and it's now costing him a per-unit-of-cleanliness price of *of*. The students as a group can be bought off at prices considerably less than *of*, and if we allow free markets (hence, free choice), this is precisely what will happen. The prof will pay students for the privilege of using their air to discharge some of his BO. He will buy them off until his control cost is just equal to their willingness to substitute other goods and services (through money) for pristine air purity. Again, this will occur at the same equilibrium price and level of cleanliness as was the case with the alternative rights assignment price *oa* and quantity *oc*.

According to this analysis, property right assignments will make no difference whatsoever in the price of pollution control, the level of pollution control, or the resources expended on pollution control. Right assignment clearly determines *who* is going to pay the shot, but not the size of the shot. This statement is absolutely true, given the assumptions both stated and implied in our free market model. These assumptions will be dropped in the next chapter, and other potential impacts of property right assignments discussed. Even with our simple model, however, we can see the potential results of several different aspects of the control problem.

If we wish to change existing levels of pollution and to maintain a free-choice society, then something must take place to change either the supply of control instruments or the demand for clean environment. Figure 3.7a–c shows the alternatives in market reactions to an increase in the supply of control instruments, a decrease in the supply of control instruments, an increase in the demand for clean environment, and a decrease in the demand for clean environment. The causes and effects of these alternatives are now discussed briefly.

An increase in the supply of control instruments will tend to move us in the direction everyone wishes to go. In Figure 3.7a, such an increase in supply is illustrated. As can be seen, this kind of shift will result in a lower per unit price of environ-

61

mental quality *and* an increase in the level of environmental quality. The shift occurs whenever there is a reduction in the cost structure facing suppliers of control instruments, including ICP_s costs, or when there is a technological improvement in the pollution control industry. Of the two positive market changes shown here (increased supply of control instruments or increased demand for clean environment), this increase in supply is the best of all possible worlds, since more quality is obtained for a lower unit cost. One can conclude, therefore, that policies tending to encourage technological improvements should be favored. True enough, but don't forget that research leading to technological improvements also has a price tag to be considered. A decrease in supply could occur if the cost of control instruments rises in relation to other goods and services (Figure 3.7b). This can happen, particularly if the types of pollution and the methods of control become more and more complex.

Increasing the demand for environmental quality will also increase the equilibrium level of quality (Figure 3.7c). In this case, however, such an increase will be associated with an increase in the price of control. Remember that several things can increase demand. What do you suppose the various campaigns against pollution are attempting to do in an economic sense? Increase demand through increased *tastes* for clean environment, of course. In other words, these campaigns are trying to get people to be more willing to *pay* to reduce pollution. Recall what we said in Chapter 1—pollution control is probably a normal or superior good. This means that increasing incomes in the country by economic growth will also increase the demand for pollution control. Here it is in the diagram. Here, again, increased material welfare would tend to increase the demand for pollution control. Increasing information (not propaganda) about the true effect of pollution can also increase the demand for control measures.

Before finishing up our chapter on the standard economics approach to markets, two terms should be mentioned. For some economists and many noneconomists, these two words hold the key to all the problems of environmental quality. One of these is *externality*. In the past few years there has been a particularly obnoxious TV commercial in which a nice plastic-looking

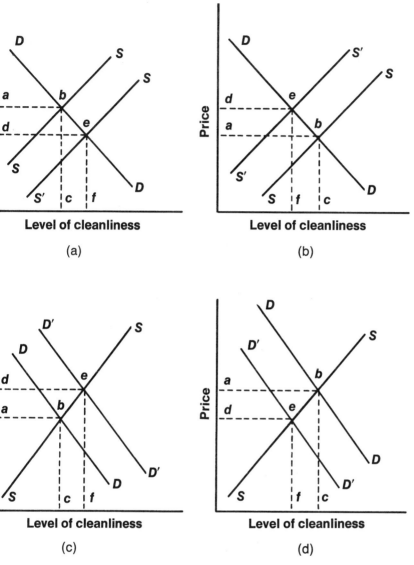

Figure 3.7 The Cleanliness Markets

middle-class hausfrau relishes great bites out of an enormous onion. Following this course of action, she's foolish enough to walk through a room full of equally plastic-looking people and give them the dragon fire at close range. Her mom and dad faint clean away. Some idiot, probably her former gigolo, dashes out to find greener pastures (so to speak); and her offspring practically wets his pants trying to escape mommy's clutches. The whole bloody scene is reenacted after Plastic Annie uses some new Magic Dragon Fire Putter Outer. This product is sort of an oral white knight and saves all the above-mentioned characters from death by suffocation. So where's the externality? Annie paid 25 cents for the onion and her willingness to pay 25 cents was based on her own enjoyment or physiological benefit from eating the thing. Having eaten it, she caused the air around her to become polluted to the extent that other people suffered loss of utility, satisfaction, pleasure, and so on. From the standpoint of the entire plastic society, the *gain* in Annie's utility from eating the onion was accompanied by a *loss* in utility by those on whom she breathed. This loss might be greater than the utility gain acquired by Annie. The externality appears if one assumes that the market for *onions* did not reflect the costs of the bad breath to everyone else. As we will see later, the externality doesn't *necessarily* exist if transactions costs are small, with property rights clearly defined and optimally assigned.

A second term that requires explanation is *public good.* A pure public good is defined as one which can be consumed or used by one person without diminishing the usefulness of the good or its availability to others. An old chestnut often used as an example is the lighthouse, marking a hazard to navigation. The services of the lighthouse are in no way diminished when an additional ship uses its lighted beacon. By the same token, it is difficult if not impossible to limit the use of the beacon service to any particular ship or ships. This is where one of the big problems comes in when traditional markets are relied upon to supply the services of public goods. When it is possible to have free riders—people who can use the good without paying for it—the inclination is to let Charlie provide it. Of course, Charlie has decided to let Joe do it, but Joe wants a free ride too, so he decides Clarence should do it, and on and on, ad infinitum.

The view of a good-looking female is also a public good. Don't get uptight, women's lib types. I said the *view* of a good-looking female. Dirty old men can look to their **heart's** content and not reduce the viewing potential for other dirty old men. The supply problem is reduced in this case, because the motivation back of the good-looking appearance is not to be viewed by dirty old men but rather by dirty *young* men. These hapless beings find themselves trapped by the viewee, which was the viewee's idea in the first place.

Many other implications can be drawn from the simple analysis presented here. We have included only the simplest of tools, but you can get a lot of insight by using them if you wish. It is probable that you will raise more questions than have been answered at this stage, and that's all right too, as long as they're the right questions. Now it's time to look in more detail at some of the simplifying (and unrealistic) assumptions we have made thus far. For some economists, the following chapter will be heresy. Oh well, you can't get *everyone* to love you anyway. Furthermore, some people's love just isn't worth the trouble (the costs are too high for the expected benefits).

4
CHAPTER

The Theory
of Crud—
With Heresy

Just to make sure that we're all on the same frequency at this juncture, think about the material we've covered thus far. In Chapter 1 we laid out some philosophical approaches, showing extreme positions on environmental quality and hinting about compromise positions that might lie in between. In Chapter 2 we discussed briefly the *technological* and natural boundaries or constraints which limit our actions in this matter. In Chapter 3 we presented what amounts to a standard economic principles attack on the problem, with the usual strong assumptions often stated or implied in economic analysis, but rarely challenged. The point, so far, is that environmental quality *is* a scarce good. To get it requires either the death of mankind or the giving up by mankind of some alternative goodies. The boundaries of some of these choices are made by nature herself, or at least by man's knowledge of nature. The boundaries of some other choices are established by man, who can change these boundaries by modifying some of the structures and institutions he has created. The impact of one of these institutions—property rights—is the primary subject of this chapter.

Some of you, recalling what you have read in the preceding

chapter, will say, "Ah ha! I told you so! If you use the market mechanism to solve environmental quality problems, you're still going to have *some* pollution, and we're against pollution!" Strictly speaking, you've got a point. The operation of the market as demonstrated in Chapter 3 usually won't eliminate *all* pollutants from the environment. It won't because most people are not prepared to pay the very high prices such elimination would incur. What the free market does do is to *optimize* the positions of the two trading partners—in this case the producers of pollutants and the sufferers from pollutants. Free markets, with the strong assumptions of perfect knowledge and zero transactions costs, mean that trade will take place one of two ways.

First, assume perpetrators hold the property rights to the resource being used for waste disposal. In this case, a free market allows sufferers to pay perpetrators to cut down the pollution they are creating. This *opportunity* for the perpetrators to earn revenue in return for pollution reduction means that they must consider the costs their pollution is imposing on the sufferers. This *opportunity cost* forces them to consider as their own internal costs, effects that would otherwise be external to their operations. If property rights are held by the sufferers, the perpetrator is forced to pay an explicit cost if he is to buy the right to use the resource in question for waste disposal. In either case, transactions will take place until the sum of the perpetrator's control costs plus the sum of the sufferers' damage costs are minimized. Further transactions mean that one party would be worse off, without the other party's gaining at least an equivalent amount. This is the optimum which our free market with perfect knowledge, assigned property rights, and zero transactions costs would produce.

Good grief! If it's that simple, let's have at it and fix the market. We'll assign property rights, get perfect information so it will work, and just forget about transactions costs. They can't be that important anyway, right? Wrong! This chapter (and it's probably the most important one in this book) is going to look at the problems our sacred old free market has in carrying on this beautifully simple operation. You might as well realize, however, that the authors are looking at it with a

68

sympathetic and (hopefully) constructive eye. We're in favor of "fixing it," not "forgetting it." We are not prepared to throw the baby out with the bath water, at least not yet; but we're bloody anxious to find out what's in the bath water that's giving baby the screaming itches.

As you've probably guessed, some more pictures must be involved if we're going to continue talking about a market. The things talked about in this chapter all tend to foul up the nice clean supply and demand analysis of the preceding chapter. There, our supply *line* and demand *line* defined boundaries as sharp as a razor between acceptable prices and quantities, and unacceptable prices and quantities, in market transactions. Everybody knew all that was important to know about the rights being marketed. Nobody had to *pay* anything for the operation of the market. Uncertainty, at least in this field, didn't exist. Everyone not only *knew,* but *knew for sure.* Property rights could be assigned to either party, which changed the exact meaning of each bound (supply and demand) but didn't change the boundaries themselves or their *unique* intersection which produced our optimal equilibrium.

As we drop these strong assumptions in the following pages, it may help you to visualize the contrast between the geometric market given in Chapter 3 and our present ones involving either/or high and different *ICP* (transactions) costs for buyer and seller. In Figure 4.1, we repeat the market diagram for our smelly professor in Lecture Room 3-A. Before (Figure 3.6), with the assumptions of perfect certainty (information) and zero *ICP* costs, our demand function looked like *DD* and our supply function like *SS*. There was an equilibrium price of *oa* and an equilibrium cleanliness level of *oc* percent. If we introduce uncertainty or high *ICP* costs, our nice clear bound-aries of supply and demand become very fuzzy and indefinite. Supply may lie in the shaded area between *SS* and *S'S'*, while demand may lie between *DD* and *D'D'*. If the degree of uncer-tainty were the same for all parties involved in the markets, the supply and demand functions would *shift* rather than become fuzzy. In this case *unique* equilibriums could still occur but always at lower than "perfect market" levels of cleanliness. One of the problems with uncertainty is that it doesn't gener-

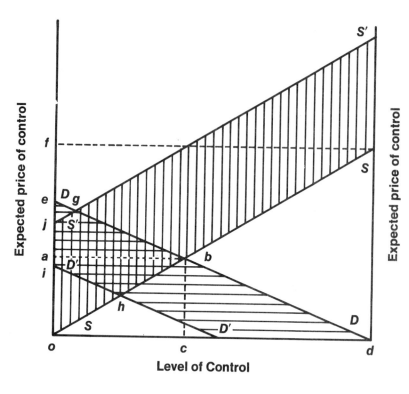

Figure 4.1 High and/or Different ICP *Costs in the Market for Clean Air in Lecture Room 3-A*

ally hit everyone the same way. This phenomenon can produce the band of possible prices and quantities illustrated by the area between *SS* and *S'S'* as well as the area between *DD* and *D'D'*. Notice now that *unique* equilibrium no longer exists; what does is merely a mass of points lying in the area *ijgbh*. Notice also that the upper boundary of supply (*S'S'*) could lie *above* the lower boundary of demand (*D'D'*), making any transaction impossible—the minimum price of the smallest quantity of control is greater than the maximum price anyone is willing and able to pay. At this point, *no* control would be generated by the free market. Another interesting point comes out of this geometry. With our perfect market, prices for buyers and sellers were identical and were known by all. Now, however, prices facing buyers and sellers may differ greatly if the *ICP* costs or uncertainties facing the trading partners are not the same. No single price will optimize the solution for everyone at the same time. At this juncture the geometry may confuse more than assist you. Read on, dear friends. If we've guessed right, it should become clearer and may help you wade through the presentation coming up.

One point should probably be stated again (it was made in Chapter 1) before we muddle on into the important business of property rights and uncertainty. We've been passing over the business of economic *equity* in a pretty loose manner, and it must be bugging the hell out of many of you. If you're a living, breathing, and *feeling* human being, you obviously are going to have opinions on who *should* pay what, what character *should* receive how much, and so on. Blessings on you! Even these miserable authors, who are making you sweat right now, have *their* ideas about the same things. Obviously, the assignment of property rights is *always* going to affect *income distribution* and therefore economic equity, even though it might not affect the *economic efficiency* of a perfect market solution. Again we remind you that just because we're separating the efficiency and equity issues doesn't mean that the equity issues are not important. *They are!* But the efficiency issues are the ones that often get neglected, particularly in an area as emotionally loaded as environmental quality. Efficiency issues are also the only ones your authors feel even partially competent to discuss.

Interestingly enough, income distribution differences can affect economic efficiency as well as equity through the income effect on the demand for a clean environment. If sufferers are always stuck with the need to pay off perpetrators, they may end up so broke that *effective* demand for a clean environment disappears. Were sufferers holding the property rights to the resource concerned, and assuming perpetrators had more wealth to blow, the income effect would *not* reduce future demand for control. Another most important effect that must be mentioned in passing is that produced by pollution on people's health. Assume it was possible to load all the air in the world with sufficient crud to kill emphysema sufferers. If the property rights to the air were vested in the sufferers, probably an infinite amount would be needed to buy the pollution rights from them. If, however, the rights were vested in the polluters, the amount the sufferers *could* pay would be limited to their wealth, incomes, and expected incomes. Presumably, this would be less than an infinite amount. Here again, changing property rights would change the prices buyers and sellers would be *willing and able* to pay or accept.

Well, onward and upward. So far, we've been yelling about property rights and their assignments. Now it's time we looked carefully at the anatomy of these rights. No study of natural resource problems can possibly be complete without knowledge of ownership patterns, because the structure of these rights is critically important to the outcome of our lives on earth.

If you're going to have exchange, you've *got to have* property rights. As we've said at least twice before, those rights are really the object of exchange processes. *They are the community's rules of the game.* Ideally, they set the standards of conduct for all members of the community. They consist of all the administrative and judicial processes, ordinances, regulations, laws, mores, and customs which limit and constrain an individual when dealing with the rest of the group. Just as the laws of the *physical world* impose technical constraints on the processes that can occur in transformation of one good into another and in exchange of one good for another, so do the laws of *property* impose constraints on these same exchange and transformation possibilities. The basic difference is that technical constraints are imposed by the unchangeable behavior of the natural world (at least as man understands it), and laws of property are constraints which the community decides to *impose on itself.* In the case of physical laws, man just ain't got no choice but to play along, hopefully understanding a bit better as time goes on. But in the case of property laws, *the rules of the game are a matter of choice.* Presumably, the choice between *sets* of rules is made on the basis of the community's expectations about the outcome of using each particular set. Each society tries to choose that set of rules which will best achieve whatever objectives it has in mind. The choice of rules will include considerations of the human skills and physical constraints that exist at the time. As these constraints and skills change over time, the rules of the game must also shift if they are to meet objectives under the new conditions.

Property, then, does not consist of a set of material objects, but rather a set of rules intended to channel and direct private behavior. Property defines the uses to which an owner may or may not put a material object, whom the owner can exclude from using the object, and to whom he may sell or transfer the object. These rules are collectively sanctioned and enforced.

The first two characteristics of property (uses and exclusions) define the authority that the sovereignty has granted to the owner to make decisions about the object's use in deriving income or satisfaction. The third characteristic defines the authority vested in the owner to exchange the object with other parties for other income or satisfaction-producing objects. A property right, therefore, assigns to particular individuals or groups of individuals final responsibility for resource use. By defining the activities individuals may perform with respect to material objects, it also specifies how individuals must behave with respect to each other. Specifically in the natural environment and with natural resources, as with any valuable good, property rights define relations between *man* and *man.* Relations between *man* and *nature* exist in property law *only* so that relations between men can be specified. Robinson Crusoe didn't need any system of property rights until ol' Friday appeared on the scene.

The key point in the preceding paragraph is that legal structures are processes for dealing with the *costs* individuals impose on each other. In every *legal* use of a material object and in every *legal* transaction between private parties, the public is always involved. It is represented by the judge, elder, or chief, who decides, or is expected to decide, every dispute over interpretation of the rules of the game. Rarely does the judge or elder proceed without adhering to that which the sovereignty has authorized by either precedent, tradition, or explicit direction. In this sense the public is involved in every transaction between two or more parties involving a material object and/or its use.

Some objects that have well-defined property rights today

were not always encompassed within the rights system. In particular, property rights in land and natural resources have undergone substantial changes in the English-speaking world during the last thousand years. Objects to which property rights attach come from two sources: the capture of goods from the natural environment and the creation of new goods by transformation of other goods from the natural environment (refer back to Chapter 2). The transformation process involves the use of human skills as well as other goods previously created (capital goods). In earliest times, people probably considered "property" to be only goods taken from nature and transformed in some way. Objects which remained in the natural environment were considered to belong to everyone. When the hide was on the back of the brontosaur, it belonged to anyone who could clobber the brontosaur. Once the beast was captured and skinned, the property right to the skin was vested in the holder, at least until someone stronger came along to challenge the right.

The accumulation of human knowledge and skills and the increased use of specialization as a means of increasing productivity of the community opened up new possibilities to obtain real income and satisfaction. A greater number of material transformations became possible, and transformation processes became increasingly long and complex. Objects in the natural environment became objects of increasing value. When these objects became valuable to more than one person in the community, rules were established defining how the objects could be used. It became necessary to establish *who* had to pay *whom* in order to use *what*.

Probably the first set of rules to be established evolved from the formation of coalitions of individuals into tribes and clans. These tribes were formed for the express purpose (among others) of excluding nontribal members from using some resource or resources which tribe members were permitted to use as they wished. Generally, the tribal member could not exchange his share of the tribe's property with another tribal member or with an outsider, because he didn't "own" anything himself. The agreement of the full tribe was necessary before any outside exchange could occur. The member could, however, put the tribal resources to any use he felt was worthwhile.

As conditions continued to evolve, as tribes became large enough to encompass whole nations, and as broad authority was vested in leaders or sovereigns, more or less central regulation of land and natural resource use became common. Prior to the fourteenth century, in the feudal state of the English-speaking world most property rights in land and natural resources were vested in the king or ruler. The overwhelming mass of inhabitants had extremely limited rights to the land they tilled and the natural resources associated with that land. The king held all and parceled out large holdings to his military aides and court favorites. These landholders, in turn, granted very limited and conditional rights to individuals under their control. Generally, the individual inhabitant was severely limited in the uses to which he could put the land, whom he could exclude from the land, and to whom he could convey his interest in the land. For example, the common farmer was often prohibited from cutting trees on the land adjoining his fields, or from letting someone else use his land, or from deeding or selling the land. The permission of the lord was required to do any of these things.

As early as the fourteenth century, substantial trade in goods and services began to take the place of personalized barter and oath. These developments, as well as changing production techniques, gradually caused exclusive individual property rights to evolve. Most resources that were not fugitive and mobile became privately held. With few exceptions, the landowner was given the right to use his property exactly as he saw fit. He could dig it up, burn it, plant it, let it lie fallow, spray it, flood it, trample it, or do anything else he wished. In the predominant and most unconditional form of property right in land, the *fee simple absolute,* the individual is presumed to have an absolute interest for as long as he wishes in something the law calls "real." This "real property" includes soil, whatever is below the soil, the use of stream waters which pass through the property, the atmosphere above the property, and as much of the air space as can be used or is needed for security.

The English jurist Coke expressed the concept of the fee

simple absolute when he said that the use rights of owners extended up to heaven and back again to hell. These include the right to prevent usage of the property by persons the owner wishes to exclude, as well as the right of the owner to sell his property to whomever he wishes. The government, be it the king of England or the United States Congress, was and still is willing to expend considerable effort to insure that the owner's will is enforced.

There has been an evolution in the property right structure for many natural resources. Common ownership has been increasingly replaced by private ownership. This evolution has been caused by man's desire to transform *natural* states and systems into forms which better serve his purposes. These transformation processes have generally used increasing levels of capital goods—machines, factories, and so on—which in turn have required *investment*. The process of investment means that people have to forgo command over goods and services in the *present* in return for command over *future* goods and services. Hence, *expectations* of future conditions and events have become an increasingly important factor in determining present decisions, particularly investment decisions. Whenever one talks of expectations, some degree of *uncertainty* is implied. If you know for sure what's going to happen, you have perfect certainty and the future is no longer in doubt. The more uncertainty can be reduced, the more future events can be accurately reflected in present decision making. From an investor's viewpoint, the more he can control future events (or things which determine these future events), the more willing will he be to invest in the future program. The institution of private property makes control over future events easier and less uncertain. It assures the investor that any property in which he invests will be controlled *by him* to a large degree. Any actions he takes in regard to the property will be effective in the manner he wishes them to be effective. Ill-defined or nonexistent property rights increase uncertainty and tend to distort capital investment programs. This is particularly significant when these investment decisions affect environmental quality, as you will see shortly.

The doctrine of fee simple absolute has been broadly applied to immobile and readily identifiable items such as land.

In other cases, however, examples of exclusive and unalienable property rights are tough to find. When a resource such as flowing air or flowing water is mobile and hard to identify, rights have generally remained vested in the sovereign. In thirteenth-century England, it was agreed that by natural law both air and water, together with the rights to use them, were the common property of all the people of a country. Publicly held resources were regarded as wild things, which any man might appropriate if he could exercise exclusive control over them. These same items might also be things-in-common, to which every man has as much right as his initiative might entitle him.

Even though sovereigns have generally retained title to such things as flowing air and flowing water, they often have *not* made precise rules about who could use them and under what conditions use could occur. Implicitly, the policy has been that such resources could be regarded as free goods. In other words, anyone could use them without charge, hindrance, or permission. If any conflicts develop between different potential users, the fights must be settled on a case-by-case basis, without reference to established property right principles. Since no one holds proper title to the air or water itself, disagreements have often been resolved by tying the use of the goods to the immobile land which the parties do own. Thus, the sufferer from air pollution might get a court to force an emitter to stop dumping junk into the atmosphere by showing that the emitter is damaging a flower garden owned by the sufferer. But because neither the receptor nor the emitter holds title to the air mass into which the junk is being dumped, *there exists no opportunity to specify the conditions of use before the waste discharge begins.*

Under circumstances in which no rules of the game exist which specify conditions of use *prior* to any actual use, the potential polluter has a distinct advantage over potential sufferers who want the quality of the resource maintained. In the absence of preexisting rules, it is the perpetrator who possesses the power to set the initial course of events. Under a system of no rules whatsoever, individual economic units who have opposing interests in the use of a resource cannot *bargain,* cannot *negotiate,* and cannot *exchange,* because they have nothing to negotiate with. In the absence of property rights, *individuals have no legal rights.* Perpetrators are not made to bear the costs of harmful activities, nor can sufferers pay to prevent them.

Let us look carefully at the case in which ownership of a scarce resource either is nonexistent or is vested in a group which specifies no rules of the game for its use. Assume that a potential polluter's decision to undertake any particular enterprise is based on his evaluation only of how it will affect him. If no rules of the game exist regarding his use of some scarce resource, he can use that resource as though it were a free good. In the absence of specified rights, sufferers from any action of the polluter will have no course of action against the polluter. The polluter need not consider the consequences of his pollution to sufferers.

Let's go to the example of an electric company with crud-producing stacks. If the householders of the area own the air rights, they can force the company to pay for polluting. The company probably won't stop polluting completely, because it is able to buy off the householders to put up with *some* pollution. This amount will be less than the pollution generated when the company considers the air to be a free good. Amazingly enough, reassigning the air rights to the company *does not make the air a free good to the company.* The reason is simple. Householders (or some of them) would be willing and able to *pay* the company to reduce the pollution levels it creates. As long as the opportunity exists to make these transactions, the company must and will regard the opportunity to be paid as a cost of using the air to remove its wastes. It is as though the company now consists of an electric division and a clean-air division. If the electric division messes up the air too much, the company will lose money, because its clean-air division ain't got nothin' to sell. The *total* company must weigh the *total* impact of its actions in order to maximize profit. Therefore, even if the air rights are assigned to the polluter, the fact that the rights *exist* along with an operating market requires the polluter to consider the impact of his actions on others. The absence of rights assignment means that the market has no way whatsoever of reflecting the total costs and benefits of

78

using the unassigned property. The market makes it worthwhile for anyone to consider as his own cost the cost his activities impose on others. If an owner of some property (such as the sovereign who owns the air and water) is hesitant to assign property rights to this good because of uncertainty about the uses to which it may be put, he can stipulate allowable uses in the exchange agreement. For example, the owner of a tract of land may be worried about the class of uses a would-be purchaser might permit. The owner can stipulate in the exchange agreement that only certain specific uses will be allowed, and any other use will void the sale. This sort of stipulation is very common in the sale of land for development and recreational areas.

An absence of property rights can have different consequences depending on whether the users of the good in question are simultaneously perpetrators and sufferers and whether depletion of the resource occurs. In other words, does the polluter suffer from his own muck or is it only dumped on others? The behavior of emitters who dump their crud into the atmosphere may differ substantially from the behavior of those who hunt wild animals. In both cases, no individual "owns" the resource (air and animals). In the air pollution case, there obviously exist sufferers that the emitters don't consider in making their decisions regarding smoke emission. These sufferers, however, are *not* other emitters. In other words, emitters do not damage each other with their pollution activities. The emitters have no incentive to initiate trade with each other. Using the air resource as a *sink* in which to dump wastes reduces the clean air available to breathers in the area, but it does not reduce one bit the amount of the air resource available to other emitters. The individual emitter will therefore go on blithely spewing his wastes into the atmosphere, totally disregarding the harm his activity is causing sufferers. He will also disregard the activities of other emitters, because their use of air affects neither his own use of the same resource nor theirs. No matter what improvements occur in the production processes or air pollution control equipment, the individual emitter will have no incentive to adopt them.

Where no rules of the game exist for hunting wild animals,

the behavior of the hunters is somewhat different from that of the air pollution emitter. The stock of the wild animals is *depletable* in that the size of the future stock depends in part on the size of the present stock. The removal of one animal from the stock by a given hunter means that the animal will not be available for capture by any other hunter. The absence of property rights will cause the hunters to disregard the costs they impose on each other. Since no individual hunter can dictate the terms on which other hunters can use the stock, it is in *no one's* interest to invest in increasing or maintaining the wild animal stock. No one finds it worthwhile to worry about the size of future stocks, because no *individual's* future wealth depends on how well *he* (alone) manages the present stocks. The individual user is in physical competition with all other users to get as large a share of the animal population as he can. There is no point in restraining the hunting or in waiting for the future, since such action merely means that others will get the forgone hunt. If one is foolhardy enough to wait for a better time, he will find that his "share" has been taken by others. By waiting or delaying, the individual finds that the costs imposed by other hunters are only accentuated, because they continue the chase. Furthermore, if there is no limit to the number of persons allowed to hunt, the depletion will be speeded by the entry of new hunters. In short, he who gets there "fustest with the mostest" gets all the beaver, oil, ground water, trees, water buffalo, alligators, and whales. Unless enforceable rules are established which specify the conditions under which hunting may occur, these wild stocks will usually be depleted, perhaps to the point of extinction. Any improvement in the technology of hunting (lumbering, mining, and so on) or any increase in consumer demand will only reduce the stocks further and faster, since the returns to the activity will increase. Hunters will intensify their efforts, and additional people will become hunters.

Limited stocks of biological creatures are not the only things to which this phenomenon occurs. The frustrating crowding of urban expressways, for example, stems from precisely the same causes as the extinction of the passenger pigeon. Nevertheless, planners continue to feign amazement when they build more "free" roads in response to congestion, only to find that the new "free" roads became congested as well.

We have already shown that assigning property rights to an individual increases his control over the good itself, including its future use. This tends to increase his ability to control future events involving the good by decreasing uncertainty, thus making investment more desirable. If property rights are ill defined or are nonexistent, uncertainty is increased by reducing the investor's ability to control both events in the future, as well as his own position within those events. Investment becomes relatively less desirable. When the good happens to be clean air or clean water, and property rights to the raw water and raw air are not defined precisely, investment in the cleanliness of these resources is a questionable action at best. At worst, it is merely money down the rat hole for the investor.

From the economy's standpoint, the absence of property rights means that the good concerned is bound to be overused. It will be treated as though it were a free good, even though such treatment imposes external costs on others. The perpetrators of pollution have no incentive to account for the costs they impose on others. Remember our smelly professor. As long as the air rights were not assigned, he could and did treat the smell-disposal abilities of the air as a free good. He overused the resource. Given assignment of air rights to either party, pollution was reduced by market operations. Either he sold the clean-air rights to sufferers or he paid the sufferers to allow *some smaller level* of BO discharge.

Uncertainty, whether it stems from poorly defined rights or any other cause, is something people would rather do without. As used here, "uncertainty" means merely that predictions about the future are not 100 percent for sure. Under this definition, *perfect certainty* almost never exists, although degrees of certainty vary over wide ranges. For most cases, the people's desire for increased certainty is intuitively obvious, particularly in the area of material goods and services. Let's look at an example less directly connected with crass materialism.

Assume it's Tuesday and Charlie wants a date for Saturday night. If Jessica is the only chick around for that night, then her acceptance or rejection of Charlie's invitation to view the midnight submarine races in Lake Michigan will involve little cost to Charlie (except for the six-pack which she would undoubtedly consume should she accept). Charlie either sits home alone or dates Jessica. The problem is that Jessica won't give him the word until late Saturday afternoon. But Clara is also on Charlie's list. From past experience, Charlie knows that the odds of Jessica's availability are about fifty-fifty. The odds for Clara's availability are about ten to one in favor. Assuming Clara and Jessica are equally acceptable to Charlie and that asking one means it will be too late to ask the other, you bloody well know who is going to get the invitation. Of course, if Jessica is a sure thing once dated and Clara's a cold fish, the decision may change. Charlie would no longer be indifferent to which one he dated. But even if Jessica is "better" than Clara, given sufficient differences in their probabilities of acceptance, Clara will still get the nod. A bird in the hand is worth two in the bush. Everything else being equal, Charlie will be a risk averter, like most people.

Men (and women) will be willing to take a particular course of action as long as no cost, implied or actual, attaches to this action. If the *potential* costs of some action (as viewed by the individual) exceed the potential gain from the action (again, as viewed by the individual), it's no dice. Assuming the date with Clara is less desirable, then any increase in the uncertainty of Jessica's acceptance will tend to lead to a less desirable solution. This is quite general. Increasing uncertainty about the future tends to lead toward less desirable decisions about the future.

Uncertainty imposes another cost on the community. This has to do with the natural tendency of individuals to hedge their bets. The old chestnut known as Murphy's law roughly states that if a particular happening is all set to go except for one thing that *could* go wrong, that thing *will* go wrong. Whether this law is correct, most people act as though it were. In other words, when faced with uncertain outcomes, people will prepare contingency plans of one kind or another. We keep our options open as long as possible, even though doing so often imposes a cost on us. Individuals expend resources to be prepared for more than one possible outcome. Given that only one outcome can actually be realized, all the resources spent for *unrealized* outcomes are irretrievably lost.

In our dating example, Charlie could have hedged his bets by asking both girls for the same date. In fact, he might have asked half a dozen on the assumption that at least one might accept. The arranging would have cost Charlie considerable time and effort, and all this effort spent on the ones he *didn't* go out with would be wasted. The other gals would have been wasted too, at least for that night, since they were mere contingency plans that proved not to be needed. Charlie might have paid a long-run cost besides, if the gals ever found out what his silly game was all about.

Again, all this shows is that increasing uncertainty increases the hedging that people will attempt. This hedging may consume resources that would not be used were uncertainty reduced.

One common means of reducing uncertainty in some areas is by individuals pooling their bets. That is, they buy insurance from specialists who, because of the large number of persons they insure, can better predict future outcomes for the *aggregated* group. In this way, each individual bears a *certain* but small cost rather than run the risk of an *uncertain* but considerably larger cost. The individual expends a relatively small amount of resources *in the present* to purchase a *contingent claim,* which, if paid at all, will be paid *in the future.* Up to a point, the greater the number of participants in the insurance scheme, the greater the benefits for all participants, since the risk can be spread among larger numbers of people. Whatever method is used to attempt reduction of uncertainty, through insurance or alternative plans, the idea is to diversify. Nevertheless, although both approaches to the reduction of uncertainty can (not will) reduce the severity of the losses individuals suffer, they can never fully negate these losses. The achievement of diversity through the use of a variety of inputs, flexible inputs, or insurance schemes still requires the expenditure of valuable resources. *The losses caused by an absence of defined property rights can never be entirely alleviated.* Insuring costs are likely to be considerably higher in a situa-

83

tion where everyone must insure against contingencies than would be the case if someone owned the resource and thus controlled the contingency being insured.

For environmental resources where property rights are poorly defined, this irreducible minimum is probably rarely, if ever, reached. One reason is the difficulty of developing insurance schemes for protection against the deterioration of the environment. Examples of insurance against predictable natural hazards can be found, but insurance against man-made hazards, such as air and water pollution or the spoiling of natural attractions, is virtually nonexistent. Thus, the only means of adjustment available to those who suffer from an absence of property rights over environmental resources is the use of a *variety of inputs* (alternative approaches) or highly flexible inputs. As an example, assume you're going to build a house in a nice, quiet suburb. Comes time to paint that little dream cottage and you are faced with a decision on what kind of paint to use. One kind is perfect for normal atmospheric conditions and will last about five years *if* there's no sulfur in the air. The other kind will last only about three years but will stand a high level of sulfur pollution. If zoning is sufficiently strict in your suburb and surrounding area, you may be fairly sure that no electric plant is going to mess up your paint. Therefore, you choose the most efficient paint for the job—the five-year, non-sulfur-tolerance one. On the other hand, if air rights are poorly defined in the surrounding area and there's a chance that some industrial smoke may wreck your paint job, you'll choose the three-year, sulfur-resistant stuff. If it was possible to buy air pollution insurance, you might buy the five-year paint while also paying an insurance premium. Similarly, a hunter of wild game to which no property rights attach will tend to use the hunting technology that will catch the most game in the shortest time—not the technology that will be the most productive in the long term. It seems unlikely that arranging inputs in this manner will do as good a job of combating uncertainty as will some type of insurance scheme. Therefore, since insurance schemes are unlikely to apply to environmental quality problems, it is reasonable to assume that losses generated by poorly defined or undefined property rights will be large compared to similarly generated losses in other types of goods. In these other types of goods, it is possible to obtain insurance for more contingencies.

The absence of insurance or contingency claims market in most environmental quality situations generates another kind of cost resulting from uncertainty. People attach different probabilities to different sets of potential future events. Similarly, people have different degrees of risk aversion. Some people love to live on the figurative high wire all their lives, while others won't even flip a coin for a cup of coffee. If the high-wire types are interested in the same goods as are the chicken types, then potential gains exist from trading in a contingency claims market. If that good in which they're interested is environmental quality, trading in the "bets" about future quality *could* improve the well-being of both risk takers and risk averters. It's the same old business. If one really hates risk, he will be willing to pay a "premium" to someone who will guarantee to cover potential damages from that risk. Similarly, if risk takers are around, they will be willing to accept premiums in return for the required guarantee. Because markets of this type are virtually impossible in the environmental-quality field, exchange possibilities of this type are also shut off. Earlier we saw that when trade was reduced from its potential in the environmental quality market, welfare was reduced. The same is true in the contingent claims market in environmental quality. Such a market could improve the community's welfare, but since it does not exist, welfare-producing exchanges are reduced. A contingent claims market *would* reveal to the world the *price of uncertainty*. Without this contingent claims market, trade can take place only in the damaged goods themselves, for example, land, flower gardens, fish. Some of those who are willing to bear uncertainty's costs are prevented from doing so, while some of those least willing must bear such costs.

On the basis of what has been said here about the costs generated by unassigned property rights through uncertainty, it would seem that all environmental quality problems could be "solved" if rights assignments could be made. If the specific conditions of use, exclusion, and transferability could be made explicit for the natural resources involved, the operation of the free market could do much in increasing economic efficiency involved in pollution issues. That is, in fact, the case. Have we then reached our final goals with this relatively unsophisticated solution? Unfortunately not, and the reason is that a unique system of property rights does not exist. The fee simple absolute system we have discussed is but one system. Each system of property rights is associated with a set of costs for establishing and maintaining its operation. Costs within the set will vary depending on the situation existing at any given time and place. Sets of costs vary as widely as the outcomes of the systems themselves. As we have noted, property is not a natural creation but a deliberate construction of a collective body. If such an institution did not exist, it would be necessary to create it. A whole spectrum of possible systems exists, as well as no system at all. The major feature that distinguishes these systems from one another is the degree of discretion they provide the holder of a property right. With the fee simple absolute, the individual owner can use or convey *completely at his own discretion* the object of the property right over a wide range of activities. At the opposite pole from the fee simple absolute, the usages and conveyances an owner may practice are always absolutely conditioned by the discretions of some other individual or group. In the one case, the owner may do as he pleases; in the other, the owner has virtually no discretionary power. In between lie a virtual infinite number of combinations of the polar cases.

The particular combination selected by a collection of individuals will depend first of all on the objectives of the community. Thus, since the YAF and SDS appear to have fairly diverse objectives, it is to be expected that the property right systems they would each choose, were they in power, would differ considerably. But objectives alone do not set the requirements for the rights system. It is probable that more than one set of property rights will accomplish the same objectives. Another choice problem therefore remains, because a selection must be made among various combinations satisfying the community's objectives. Usually, this choice will be made on the basis of *minimizing the resources* which must be expended to establish and operate the system. These resources consist of expenditures on informational, contractual, and policing services required by a given property right system. In other words, for a given set of objectives, the problem is to find that property right structure which minimizes *ICP* costs. The lower the *ICP* costs, the greater the opportunities to gain from the process of exchange. Every time resources are expended on *ICP* costs, those resources are lost for other productive and desirable ends. The lower the *ICP* costs, the smaller the level of resources thus expended.

Under this principle, the existence of common property in a community may well be a matter of explicit choice. The sovereignty may have found that the *ICP* costs of establishing a system of *individual* property rights in certain objects would be too great in relation to the expected benefits, given the sovereignty's objectives. An extreme example of this conscious choice of common property is found in some of the "flower communities" around the country. Many of these communes consist of people who have renounced the pleasures of the flesh associated with crass old "commercial" goods. One might argue that there's been more *substituting* than *renouncing,* but that's neither here nor there at the moment. The point is that a community living with very few goods and services because it doesn't value such goods and services very highly might well be expected to adopt a common property approach rather than use a market system for allocation. Even in this relatively small community, the *ICP* costs would probably be too large to make private property worthwhile.

There are three sets of circumstances where the net benefits from the establishment of *any* system of property rights appear nonexistent (or negative). The first set occurs whenever a good is not scarce. By "not scarce" we mean that everyone can consume all he desires of the item without using a unit anyone else could conceivably ever want. Because the good isn't scarce, the expenditure of resources to establish a system of property rights serves no valid economic purpose. At one time, the air and many wild creatures were thought to fit this category. Our flower children's culture is an example, not because other goods they hold have no value to people outside the commune, but because, according to their values, such goods are unessential and therefore not scarce. Today, it is difficult to think of an environmental resource that can properly be regarded as not scarce.

A second set of circumstances that produce prohibitively high ICP costs is when the specification and defense of the property rights over some object are very costly. That is, the cost of control over the use of the property is high. Consider the problems likely to occur if one tries to establish a fee simple absolute system in the earth's atmosphere. The sovereign will identify a distinct air mass which will then be made available to private individuals on some basis or other. The sovereign's task is really rugged. The object of the property right, the air mass, is highly mobile and is not defined with respect to a unique location. Also, a given air mass's natural characteristics can vary significantly according to meteorological and temperature conditions and to the type of covering on the land underlying the mass. For example, moisture content of the atmosphere can vary with the amount of sunlight, the amount of land surface water present, and the configuration of the land in the vicinity. With or without the entry of man-made pollutants, the object in which the property right is held will differ from one location to another. In Maine a property right in a pink Cadillac with blue tail fins remains a property right in an identical Cadillac in Los Angeles (although the owner of the property may change characteristics between the two locations). The auto is readily identifiable by its coloring, scars, and serial number on the engine block. These characteristics do not change with location. But imagine trying to identify several distinct air masses and to understand the changes in their natural make-up as they shift location. For quite obvious reasons, no sovereign has seriously undertaken this task.

Several other natural resources have the same problems as do air masses. It is very costly for example to distinguish one mass of water from another in a river. In fact, bodies of water and air, particularly air, are difficult to perceive in tiny bits. Each mass blends into every other mass, so one is virtually indistinguishable from the other. It is apparent, therefore, that a fee simple absolute system of property rights in air and water resources would be extremely expensive and perhaps even technically impossible to establish.

Recognizing these difficulties, many sovereigns have tied fee simple absolute rights of air and water use to unique locations. That is, the right is assigned to a fixed geographical place instead of to the air or water mass itself. The landowner has the right to use any transient air or water passing over, under, or through the property while it is within the owner's boundaries.

Tying property rights in air and water masses to specific locations does help the identification problem. Nevertheless, it is unlikely that a fee simple absolute system of rights in air and water will be chosen by a community, because it would be difficult to enforce the right.

Assume that such a fee simple absolute system has been established and that the rights have been parceled out to the respective landowners in the area. It is now the task of each proud owner to identify violations of his right and to attempt to prevent them. Detection requires observation and measurement as well as ability to associate the violation with the violators. Consider yourself a homeowner and a holder of fee simple absolute air and water rights in the San Bernadino Mountains at the east end of the Los Angeles basin. One day you wake up with eyes burning, chest hurting, and a hack sounding like the plague's death rattle. Smog has invaded your property and violated your right. In response, you call the person who's supposed to be responsible for policing air rights. He shows up (several hours later) with a mess of expensive monitoring equipment to establish what your aching body already knows—you've got smog. Since there are a limited number of inspectors and a limited number of expensive monitoring machines, several other violations had to go unchecked while Charlie observed your alleged violation. After several hours of goofing around, Charlie confirms the fact that you've got it. All you have to do now is identify the violators and make them pay whatever penalties are attached to using someone's property without his consent.

There are several million smog-producing automobiles in

the Los Angeles basin few of which are in exactly the same spot at the same time every day. Do you want to sue the whole bunch of them? Lots of luck! Even if you could exclude the car owners from using your right, there would still be another problem. It's cost you a bundle, but you've succeeded in getting clean air over your half-acre—and John's half-acre, and George's half-acre, and Beulah's half-acre. Know something? Those lousy leech neighbors would let you pick up the tab while they enjoy all the benefits of *your* antipollution investment without paying a cent. You could yell at them to stop breathing the air you made pure, but it probably wouldn't do any good. Unless you can exclude free riders from your antipollution efforts, the air right you possess over your house is worthless, to you and *even to your leech neighbors.* The cost of enforcing the right is too great. Property rights that aren't defensible are worthless.

Similar results would occur even if automobile drivers are given the right to emit as many fumes as they wish. Conceivably, each sufferer from air pollution can strike a bargain with the drivers who are contributing to the suffering. Assuming the drivers have no reason to blackmail sufferers, the sufferers face the same problem identifying those drivers causing the harm as when they hold the rights to the clean air. Apparently, any system of fee simple absolute in air rights puts all the cards in the hands of the polluters.

The policing problem would be much simpler if there were just one giant machine creating all the smog. There would be no question about who was producing the crud, although, of course, you'd still have to actually measure it in various locations. If the clean-air lovers held the property rights, they could insist that the monster smogger compensate them for damages. If the smogger held the property rights, the air lovers could purchase clean air from him. Though some such exchanges would probably occur, it is unlikely that *all* worthwhile exchanges would take place. The reason is again to be found in the indivisible nature of the air resource. No single clean-air lover will be able to bargain with the smogger without simultaneously affecting other clean-air lovers. If a single clean-air lover buys clean air from the smogger, he will also be buying clean air for his fellow lovers whose properties adjoin his own. If the rights belong to the smogger and if he buys pollution rights from one clean-air lover, it is probable that he will also pollute the property of adjacent property owners as well as the character from whom he bought the right.

The point of the preceding paragraph is that the indivisibility of the air resource is such that, even in the absence of high informational and policing costs, the agreement of many parties must be obtained before a bargain can be struck which includes all worthwhile exchanges. One individual's enjoyment of clean air in no way reduces the availability of clean air to other clean-air lovers. Once the clean air has been made available, it makes no economic sense to attempt to exclude anyone from breathing it. In this sense, clean air is a public good. A problem is introduced only when the provision of clean air is dependent upon the willingness of clean-air admirers to pay the shot. If one guy pays, they all get the benefit. Therefore, one waits for the other to pay, who waits for the other to pay, and so on. If nobody pays, nobody gets clean air. Everybody hopes to obtain the free ride. Mutually advantageous trades are not arrived at, because each clean-air lover is seeking as much of the free ride as possible. Nevertheless, once clean air is provided, exclusion of anyone is wasteful—unless it is necessary to obtain information on the value of clean air.

For all the preceding reasons, a fee simple absolute system of property rights in the atmosphere as well as in many other environmental resources probably means that quality deterioration would be especially severe. The cost of acquiring information necessary to establish the right, the cost of carrying out exchanges once the right is established, and the cost of policing the right all mean that the right, to the extent that the individual values a clean environment, offers little contribution to satisfaction or production. It therefore has little if any market value.

The apparent inability of the fee simple absolute system of property rights to allocate efficiently many environmental resources implies that some alternative system of property rights must be employed. In general, these alternative forms require some forgoing of complete individual discretion in decision making in order to reduce *ICP* costs and the uncertainties these costs generate. Of course, as has been noted, *ICP* costs may be so high that the existence of no property right system whatsoever is worthwhile. It may also be true, however, that placing rigid restrictions on individual discretion or placing authority in central bodies *can* (not will) generate outcomes that are more optimal than the market with high *ICP* costs and free rider problems. Simultaneously, these systems might have lower *ICP* costs than any other alternative system. If the central body makes some good guesses about which exchanges the decentralized system failed to allow, then resource allocation can be improved. Just because this is *possible* does not mean it will automatically occur. Planners and others in authority in the planning body must be provided with the incentives (positive and negative) to insure that they will seek optimal allocations.

We shall return to many of these questions in Chapter 6, where the properties of alternative means of pollution control are discussed. Right now, you're going to get a look at that real world everyone talks about. Hopefully, you will see the relevance of the concepts and ideas developed thus far.

5
CHAPTER

A Case
of Crud

Madison Avenue generally does a pretty good job of making some crummy tourist trap look like paradise. The central highlands region of Florida east of Tampa is an exception. The area is just as beautiful as the ad agents predict. Sunshine, palm trees, oranges, and recreational facilities abound in towns and around the hundreds of clear lakes in the area. Many travelers have even suggested that in *this* area man had enhanced rather than destroyed natural beauty. The towns are well spaced throughout the region and are not overrun by tourists. Long rows of citrus trees have replaced the brush on thousands of acres of rolling countryside. The swampy edges of lakes near towns have been filled, but those away from population centers have generally been left alone. Pastures cover thousands of acres of drained marshland. The seemingly incompatible industries of tourism, citrus production, and beef cattle culture work in harmony to provide an outstanding example of compatibility in highly specialized land uses.

However, one section of this Polk County area hasn't always had this sweetness and light bit between various economic interests. About fifty miles southwest of Orlando and thirty miles east of Tampa is a four-hundred-square-mile area lying in western Polk County and eastern Hillsborough County. Since the early 1950s, a scarcity of clean air has caused some major adjustments in the area's economy. There has been a serious conflict between those who wish to use the region's air for life support purposes and those who wish to use the same air to dispose of waste materials. On the life support side of the controversy stand the citrus and cattle interests; on the waste disposal side stands a substantial phosphate fertilizer manufacturing industry. Each of these industries forms a twelve-month-a-year base on which the area's economy is built. Each has a long history dating from the latter part of the nineteenth century. Each considers the unique climate and environment of the area to have precisely the characteristics needed for its own industry to flourish.

In the latter part of the nineteenth century, the citrus industry in Florida was centered about one hundred miles north of Polk County. A disastrous series of freezes virtually wiped out citrus during the 1894–1895 crop year. Searching for better protection from future cold spells, growers took note of the plentiful lakes, rolling hills, and deep sandy soils which cover much of Polk and Hillsborough counties. These attributes, combined with the more southerly location, served to reduce substantially the probabilities of frost damage. Since the initial development during this period, the area's citrus industry has expanded to the point that it's crop value in the mid-1960s approached fifty million dollars per year. One quarter of the Florida production and nearly 15 percent of the nation's citrus fruit came from this small area. About 150,000 acres of citrus groves had a volume of production equal to slightly over three fourths of the combined citrus production of every other growing area outside the State of Florida. The region has produced as much citrus in one year as the entire State of California.

In the early and mid-1960s, mature and healthy citrus groves were selling for as much as $4000 an acre and up. Land suitable for citrus culture, but unplanted, was commonly selling for $300 per acre. A fairly large number of groves were owned by retired people who had invested their life's savings in these groves, hoping to receive sufficient earnings to make their retirement days enjoyable.

The semitropical climate, easy access to Eastern markets,

and low unit costs of production have also brought about the development of a substantial beef cattle industry. The majority of these enterprises are medium-to-large ranches with herds as large as 1500 head. Most of the cattle are a hybrid originating from the Indian Brahman breed, which is particularly well adapted to the humid subtropical climate of Florida. These cattle ranches provide the primary, and sometimes only, income for their owners. Since there is no need to move the herds from summer to winter ranges or to import large quantities of winter feeds, Polk County's cattle population has reached a level of from 80,000 to 120,000 head, fed on approximately 500,000 acres of grassland. According to available data, however, the beef cattle industry is not particularly lucrative. The 1964 U. S. Department of Agriculture census indicates that beef producers in this area averaged sales of only $4.26 per acre of pastureland. Land suitable for grazing only was rarely sold for amounts in excess of $150 per acre.

The presence of both citrus and cattle can probably be mostly explained by the advantageous location provided by Polk County. This same locational advantage probably explains the presence of the area's major polluter as well, the phosphate fertilizer industry. The area contains the world's largest and richest phosphate rock deposits. Since 1894, the Florida phosphate industry has provided over 50 percent of the nation's phosphate rock, and now provides over 75 percent of this mineral. The value of the rock at the mine alone amounts to over one hundred million dollars annually, thus reflecting the productivity of Florida's phosphorus elements to the nation's agricultural production. These fertilizers make substantial contributions toward feeding the world's hungry.

For more than fifty years, the area's beef, citrus, and phosphate industries enjoyed peaceful coexistence, while each did its thing in satisfying man's hunger pangs. Cattle became as fat as one could reasonably expect in the local climate. Citrus groves bore their fruit regularly. The phosphate industry mined its rock and loaded it aboard trains and ships to be transported throughout the eastern United States and the world. But the late 1940s and early 1950s brought a drastic change in the nature of the local phosphate industry, resulting in a rapid increase in the operation of phosphate fertilizer *manufacturing* (as opposed to just mining) plants in the Polk County area. The major processing carried out in these new plants was the manufacture of so-called concentrated or triple-super phosphate fertilizer and phosphoric acid.

When triple superphosphate (TSP) was first manufactured in the early part of the twentieth century, it was not widely accepted in the nation's agriculture. Farmers, unaware of the tremendous productive capacity of the product, were suspicious of its effect on soils. The advent of World War II, however, brought tremendous pressures for increased food production. This, in turn, caused a rapid depletion in the already low levels of soil phosphate in the nation's farm belt. The rapid rate of depletion increased further by the introduction of several different Federal farm programs that attempted to limit the quantity of land farmers could use to produce crops. These limitations increased the incentives for farmers to use high-yield fertilizers on the remaining land they operated. Their idea was to get more output out of the land which remained in production so that their output could remain the same or could even increase. This clearly wasn't the government's idea or goal for the programs. Anyway, the demand for TSP increased dramatically; and in order to meet this increased demand, phosphate fertilizer companies increased their output of TSP in an equally dramatic fashion. Because a ton of TSP requires twice as much phosphate fertilizers, transport costs can be cut a great deal by locating the factories near the mines rather than near the farmers. For the same reason, steel mills are located near coal fields and meat packers near ranches. The Polk County area's daily production of TSP climbed from 850 tons in 1949 to an average of 2500 tons in 1959 and to a daily average of 8500 tons in 1966.

The "wet process" of manufacturing TSP is employed in the Polk County area. In this process, phosphate rock is treated with sulfuric acid so as to obtain phosphoric acid and gypsum. The phosphoric acid is used to treat more phosphate rock. Chemical reactions take place in both stages of the process as well as in the curing stage which follows, thus increasing the plant nutrient value from rock concentration of 6 to 8 percent to 50 percent in the finished fertilizer.

In addition to the valuable phosphorus nutrient, the raw rocks contain from 3 to 5 percent fluorine by weight. During the chemical processes, large amounts of fluorine can be liberated in the form of both gaseous and particulate fluorides, the compound form of fluorine. By far the greatest proportion of this liberation occurs during the second treatment stage and in the storage or curing stage that follows. Those liberated fluorides which are not somehow captured are emitted into the atmosphere. Given sufficiently large emissions, the result is air pollution.

In the early fifties, cattlemen and grove owners began to notice a general deterioration in the health of their animals and trees. At first, the cattlemen attributed their losses to a worm infestation, while the grove owners placed the blame on nutritional deficiencies of the area's sandy soils. Subsequent investigation showed, however, that the cattle had symptoms of fluorosis, and the citrus showed leaf damage often attributable to the presence of gaseous fluorides. One old codger, noting the association between phosphate plants and unhealthy cattle, is reputed to have accused the phosphate companies of giving the animals hoof and mouth disease. Among agricultural animals, beef cattle have very high susceptibility to fluorine toxicosis. If the animal consumes the toxin in forage containing fluorine concentrations greater than 40 parts per million (by weight), it experiences a progressive deterioration in health. The initial symptoms consist of a loss in appetite, and in body weight and in a mottling of the animal's teeth. Milk production can also be affected. If uncontaminated forage is substituted at this stage, the animal will recover, with the only deleterious effect having been a temporary reduction in his growth rate. But if substitute forage is not provided, the fluoride, owing to its affinity for calcium, will affect the animal's joints and skeletal structure. At this stage, water intake increases markedly, vomiting occurs along with bloody diarrhea, movement becomes painful and unsteady, perhaps with the animal being forced to lie spread-eagle on the ground. Finally, lumps and bony spurs appear at several points on the skeleton, and the animal's joints will stiffen to the point of immobility. Now the process is irreversible. Self-imposed starvation and finally death conclude it. These same effects take place if the animal is subjected to a single massive dose of fluoride in a short time interval.

Citrus is classed among plants that are moderately susceptible to damage from airborne fluorides. Most soils contain moderate amounts of fluoride (fluorine is the world's thirteenth most common element), but the evidence indicates that fluorides taken in through roots are relatively water insoluble and so have little effect on the plant. There is also no evidence that airborne fluorides reach the soil in any substantial amounts. Thus, if fluorides are to harm a plant, they must get to it through the plant's leaves, and the leaves of citrus trees are particularly good absorbers of airborne fluorides. Experiments indicate that air containing 5 to 16 parts per billion (by volume) will adversely affect a citrus leaf's photosynthesis or food-manufacturing processes as well as its ability to use the food it does manage to manufacture. The number of fruits produced on each tree, the weight of each fruit, and its vitamin C content also appear to be adversely affected. Finally, an undesirable thickening of the fruit's rind occurs.

During the late 1950s and early 1960s, sampling programs of the area's atmosphere pinpointed some locations where the fluoride content rarely got below 10 parts per billion from November through April. Levels have occasionally reached 50 parts per billion during these months. At the same time, another sampling program discovered locations where pasture grasses accumulated fluoride concentrations in excess of 200 parts per million over a four-week period, with concentrations greater than 100 parts per million being common.

It was in these winter and early spring months that the Polk County area's air pollution problem actually centered. Occasional temperature inversions in which the upper levels of air mass are warmer than the lower levels several hundred feet from the ground greatly reduced the air's self-cleaning ability. Air masses often act perversely and reverse directions. Thus the same fluoride-bearing air may pass over a given site two or more times. In addition to producing the unfavorable air conditions, the TSP companies attempted to increase their production during these months, because over 70 percent of the nation's fertilizer sales occur from January through May. All these factors caused fluoride concentrations in the air mass to be much higher in the winter and early spring than in the summer and fall. Areas in which pasture grasses contained fluoride concentrations above the level of 40 parts per million could expand to five hundred square miles in winter as compared to July lows of sixteen to twenty square miles. Unfortunately, these same winter and early spring months were the very months in which the cattle and citrus industries were most likely to suffer serious pollution damage. Cattle, feeding on grasses with comparatively low nutrient value, were less able to resist outside stresses which could impair their health. In the early spring months, new growth on the citrus trees begins to appear which is much more readily damaged by airborne fluorides.

Prior to 1959, the phosphate companies appeared to have had things pretty much their own way. The amount of fluorides they dumped into the atmosphere increased steadily until, by 1959, it had reached a record maximum of fourteen million pounds annually. Before the entry of the TSP plants into the picture, there was no particular need for the citrus or cattle farmers or anyone else to worry about ownership of the rights to use the atmosphere. Except for occasional attempts by citrus growers to protect their trees from frost or freeze by burning smoke pots, there was no reason to fear air pollution. Since no property rights had been established in the atmosphere, the phosphate plants could treat the air's waste disposal abilities as a free good. Prior to the arrival of the TSP plants, no identifiable and defensible system of property rights in the atmosphere had evolved, because there had been no economically valid reason for such a system. The fee simple absolute in land applied as readily to the phosphate companies as it did to the cattle and citrus farmers. Since the phosphate companies were not harming one another with their emissions, they had no incentive to work out a mutually agreeable arrangement. The status quo was already as agreeable as anything could be from their point of view. They knew *with certainty*, whatever their production plans, that they could release practically any amount of waste materials into the air with little prospect of having to bear a cost. The cattlemen and growers, in contrast, were subject to quite severe uncertainty. Their production plans were now dependent not only upon what they decided to do, but also upon what the phosphate companies decided to do.

For example, if a cattleman decided to feed his cattle on grass throughout the year, he would have very high and happy cattle. (Sorry about that). He would be less certain about the weight gains such a program would produce, because one factor influencing the weight gain would be the intake of fluorides. The amount of this intake depended upon the production plans (hence emissions) of the TSP companies. In a similar manner, a citrus grower who decided to irrigate his trees at certain intervals could not be sure of the effectiveness of his irrigation, because he could not know the fluoride dosages to which his trees would be exposed in the crop year. Cattlemen and citrus growers were in tough shape. Before the TSP plants, all they had to worry about was crop prices, growing costs, freezes, frosts, bugs, fungi, and a few other minor problems. Now they had to worry about air pollution dosages as well—dosages which were unpredictable as to degree. The severity of this uncertainty was intensified by the absence of any organized insurance agreements that would spread risk or exchange differences in risk aversion.

Even in the absence of such insurance schemes, the farmers did have four alternatives open to them other than the obvious one of suffering in silence. All four alternatives involved *cost*. First of all, the farmers (receptors) could reduce damage by employing inputs or taking actions serving to make them less susceptible to pollution damage. However, if the cattlemen were to continue to produce beef and if the citrus growers were to continue to produce fruit, economically realistic means of reducing damages had to be found. These means were both limited and extremely expensive. For cattlemen, the alternatives were to periodically substitute feeds low in fluorides for the polluted grasses. They could also transport the cattle to pastures where grasses were relatively low in fluorides. Both courses of action required heavy expenditures compared to the normal feeding pattern, but many cattlemen did resort to both of these alternatives. Citrus growers were in tougher shape. A mature citrus tree doesn't lend itself to transportation very easily, nor are there any practical ways to change the atmosphere around the tree. (Maybe put each tree in a giant bell jar, or better yet, build airtight astrodomes over all the groves.) In an extreme case, the grower could cut down his tree and grow something less susceptible to damages. As a *citrus* grower, he could not make such an adjustment in order to solve the problems imposed upon him by pollution.

A second alternative open to the receptors was to go to court. This ploy was attempted occasionally, but in very few cases was it successful. Among the more notable successes was a $208,000 judgment against a single phosphate company on behalf of cattlemen and citrus growers located within a mile of the plant. Generally, however, legal avenues could not provide the sufferers with much assistance.

The common law, as we have noted, generally gives the owner of a site strong claim to having clean air above that site.

> Title to land gives the owner the right to impregnate the air upon and over the same with such smoke, vapor, and smells as he desires, provided he does not contaminate the atmosphere to such an extent as to substantially interfere with the comfort or enjoyment of others, or injure the use of their property. But air is movable, and constantly flowing from the premises of one to those of another, and hence when it becomes thickly impregnated with putrid substances, it necessarily flows onto the adjacent premises in one direction or another . . . the business is lawful, but such interruption and destruction is an invasion of private rights, and to that extent unlawful. It is not so much the manner of doing as the proximity of such a business to the adjacent occupant which causes the annoyance. [Pennoyer vs. Allen, 56 Wis. 502, 14 N.S. 609 (1883).]

In other words, what is a sin is not a sin if it is committed in the right place. More importantly, it is up to the owner of the adjacent property to show that he has been *sinned against.* Even though the law stated that receptors had every right to have the air over their property completely free of putrid substances, it was up to the receptors to show that putrid stuff was in fact present in this air. After showing this, the sufferers, according to the law, would then have to show that the phosphate companies were responsible for the putrid substance.

Finally, unless it could be shown that the phosphate companies were acting in concert, the receptor would have to identify the specific company or companies that were pumping the crud over his particular piece of ground. He might even have to identify how much *each* company contributed to the total mess. And, of course, along with all these problems the sufferer must prove that the substances he is calling putrid are indeed putrid. He would have to prove "beyond a reasonable doubt" that the substances had caused him damage.

Think what just the establishment of fluoride damage involves. Remember, we are dealing with an element, fluorine, in a gaseous or fine particulate form. Merely to establish its presence in the air requires fairly sophisticated chemical analysis. Even after the presence has been demonstrated, one must show that the fluorine, and not some other stress, caused symptoms of the damage concerned. Usually, a number of stresses will produce symptoms closely or exactly similar to the symptoms produced by fluorides. There are, in other words, multiple causes for a particular symptom. In the Polk County case, fluoride damages to citrus trees are most readily observed in the yellowing of the tree's leaves. There is little idea, however, of the relation between degree of yellowing and the tree's ability to produce fruit, because several other stresses can also cause leaves to yellow—for example, too much irrigation, improper fertilizers, other disease. The severity of these stresses and of the fluoride effects is thought to vary with various meteorological and seasonal conditions. It is up to the court to pull all the strands apart, so that the proportionate effects of the fluorides can be assessed. In those cases which actually did reach the courtroom, the phosphate companies had no difficulty finding "scientists" from assorted institutions of learning who would dutifully recite all the possible causes of leaf yellowing and crop losses. Even if the citrus grower had complete records of all his grove operations, it was not difficult for the phosphate companies to confound the issue. The burden of proof lay entirely on the grove owners, not the phosphate companies. All the phosphate companies had to do was to raise a reasonable doubt by citing multiple possible causes. The grove owners—and they alone—had to show that these other possible causes were not responsible for the damage in question.

It is readily seen that the position of the receptor before the bar is very weak. In addition, the legal costs he has to pay increase the comparative disadvantage vis-à-vis the companies. Large corporate emitters like the phosphate companies maintained salaried legal staff and/or legal staffs on retainer whose pay continued whether or not they were in court. In other words, the *additional* costs to the companies of exercising every legal gimmick in the book were very low. In contrast, legal costs to the small grove owner were out of pocket and potentially staggering. All these factors produced uncertainties which were further magnified by the usual vagueness of applicable legal standards. Concepts—such as reasonable use, utility of conduct, gravity of loss—all cut into the ability of the farmers to employ the courts to control the companies' invasion of their property rights. The farmers' atmospheric property rights were not subject to the same protection as property rights in, say, their automobiles. The state provides police to prevent attempts to steal their cars, and even lawyers (district attorneys) to prosecute car thieves when caught. Although the cattlemen and the growers pay taxes to support these services, the total cost is shared by the entire community. To protect their air rights, farmers had to pay the *full cost*.

It was apparent that fun and games in the courtroom of Polk County wasn't going to help the sufferers in this case to any appreciable degree. They could, however, attempt a third alternative, namely, bargaining directly with the phosphate companies. But the difficulties they faced taking this course of action were similar to those faced in the legal approach. Several hundred cattlemen and growers were potentially affected by air pollution. At most, there were eleven phosphate companies and less than twenty distinct phosphate processing plants. The companies included multimillion-dollar corporations bearing such names as Swift, Armour, American Cyanamid, and subsidiaries of various international oil corporations such as Mobil. The cattlemen and citrus growers, for the most part, were one-man operations or very small companies. No one receptor could afford to make a deal with a phosphate company which would result in a meaningful reduction in the company's emissions. Such reductions would have cost the company tens, or hundreds, of thousands of dollars. Given receptor-owned air rights, the amount the receptor would have required to allow the companies pollution rights was probably considerably larger than the amount he would have been willing *and able* to pay the emitters to reduce emissions, had rights been vested in the latter. The individual cattleman or grower was usually not well-to-do and had other needs for his available resources—like keeping a roof over his head.

Of course, receptors could have banded together for the purposes of funding and bargaining with the companies. This approach would probably have produced at least some useful transactions. A good many receptors would undoubtedly have sat on the sidelines in the hope of getting a "free lunch" from their colleagues' efforts. But even apart from the free-rider problem, the *ICP costs* of bargaining faced by any cooperating group of receptors would seem to have been overwhelming. First of all, they would have to have a fairly accurate idea of the damages the fluoride air pollution was causing them so that they would not pay the companies more than the value of such damage. Then, they would have to determine for *each individual location or receptor* each company's contribution to the pollution. Failure to do this would mean potential payments to companies who were causing little, if any, pollution. Imagine the difficulties in pulling this deal off! Professional meteorologists with all kinds of expensive equipment would have a field day. Finally, even if a group of receptors did manage to reach an agreement with the companies, they would still have to police levels of air pollution emissions to insure compliance with the agreement. The state would provide these policing services only if receptors simultaneously used resources to pressure (politically) the state to perform them. If the receptors found that the companies were not adhering to the agreement, the courts would come back into the picture, with all the difficulties of proof and expense discussed previously. Thus, at least in the Polk County case, the bargaining alternative seemed even less realistic than initially attempting to defend receptor property rights in the courts.

By the mid-1950s, the situation for the sufferers had become acute. Citrus growers found that the value of their groves had decreased by more than $150 per acre, while cattlemen watched the value of their pastureland drop about $20 per acre. In other words, the market indicated an average loss in value of about 10 percent on pastureland and 5 percent on citrus groves.

In response to this worsening situation and recognizing the high costs of either bargaining or legal means, a group of receptors got together to employ a fourth alternative way of getting to the phosphate companies. The means employed by this small group were *political.* They raised hell in the newspapers, got the papers to take their problem as a righteous moral issue, got the federal government interested, and finally made local and state politicians take notice of them. A scene showing a sad-looking cow with ribs like a bird cage, bony spurs sticking out of its flanks, and down on its knees struggling to get up became one of Florida's most frequently reprinted pictures. In the publicity, the animal's sorry shape was always attributed to fluoride ingestion caused by phosphate company air pollution. In the meantime, you can be sure that pressures of a less public nature were being exerted in the political arenas.

Responding to the obviously mounting public concern for Polk County's problem, the state legislature authorized, in 1958 the formation of a state-supported air pollution control district. In effect, the state gave this district the right to specify the uses to which the local air resources could be put and who could use them. It therefore shifted from the parties to the control district the property rights in the air resource over all the parties' lands. The organization was also provided funds with which to police whatever rules it promulgated. Since the receptors' use of the air resource did not materially affect the resource's value to others, the resulting rules of use fell primarily on the phosphate companies. Among the rules attempted were standards specifying the maximum quantities of fluorides pasture grasses could contain and the types of equipment the companies could use in their production processes. It was found, however, that such rules were extremely hard to enforce. The district could not always be sure that equipment was being used in accordance with its directives. Furthermore, though receptors constantly and correctly pointed out that the grass-land standard was being exceeded at many locations, the control district had no legally acceptable set of criteria by which it could assign responsibility to *individual* phosphate companies. The following statement by the district director reflects the problems thus caused:

> The old 40 ppm regulation was not enforceable. We have spent too much time and money just developing knowledge that a violation of this regulation existed. It has been impossible to determine who or how many of the plants were in violation. When we find a violation, then we must prove who caused that. This is very difficult; which or how many of the companies caused that fluorine to be put in that grass. All we can do is present . . . that this grass is over 40 ppm, but we cannot prove who did it. Due to this, we have been badgered for the past four years something terrible [sic].

Nevertheless, in spite of the extreme expense and/or impossibility of enforcing these standards even moderately well, the district's concern in this matter needed only to be short run. In the longer run, the district was able to present the phosphate companies with a rather expensive choice: either buy up large chunks of receptor lands which were being polluted, or get fluoride emissions down to what was termed "minimum technologically feasible levels." In effect, the district told the companies that they would not be allowed to release fluorides into the atmosphere unless they had purchased the right to do so from those owning the land on which the fluorides were being dumped. Thus, after 1958, the companies attempted to find that combination of land purchases and control efforts which was a *least-cost combination,* given the options they had available. In 1958 and 1959, the phosphate companies were dumping each year more than fourteen million pounds of fluoride into Polk County's atmosphere. By 1961, this figure was down to ten and one-half million pounds, and in 1964 it was cut to less than five million pounds. During this same period, the industry's production capacity and usage of fluorine-bearing rock doubled.

The options available to the companies shifted from the sufferers (the cattlemen and growers) to the would-be perpetrators of the deterioration (the companies) the burden of initiating actions to change air quality. Now, the companies had to pay the farmers in order to bring about changes in atmospheric quality, rather than the other way around. As a result, after 1958, many knowledgeable owners of pasture land (and a few grove owners) were able to capture a substantial portion of the value of the air resource to the phosphate companies as a means of waste disposal.

When a potential buyer dealt with an owner of pasture land, the minimum price he could expect to pay would be the land's value *with* expected pollution levels. As noted earlier, this value rarely exceeded $150 per acre. The maximum price a phosphate company could be expected to pay would be the same as the maximum price a pasture owner could hope to receive. It would have cost any given company a known amount to reduce its emissions to those of minimal technological feasibility. This cost minus the amount the companies had already paid to buy land would set the amount and therefore the price companies would be willing to pay for further pasture land purchases, assuming that the given company also knew how much (and what) land other companies would be purchasing. The actual selling price in each transaction depended upon the pasture owners' knowledge of the companies' alternatives. In any case, from 1958 to 1964, pasture lands subject to pollution damage sold for an average of anywhere from $7 to $40 per acre *more* than pasture lands not subject to pollution. Many examples of unimproved pasture land selling for more than $250 per acre can be found within the pollution area during the 1958–1964 period.

For citrus lands, the citrus growers' asking prices of from $2000 to $4000 per acre appeared to be generally higher, in spite of damages, than the prices companies were willing to pay. The growers, therefore, continued to suffer some losses, although the magnitude of these losses was reduced from an average of 5 percent of an unpolluted grove's value to less than 2 percent.

When one considers the costs of controlling fluoride emissions in the phosphate plants, it becomes evident that the companies found their land purchase option, particularly pasture land, very attractive. In 1958 and 1959, when the plants were annually releasing into the air more than fourteen million pounds of fluorides, these emissions constituted only 5.1 percent of the fluorides that initially entered the production process. That is, during the most severe pollution period, the companies were still controlling, in one way or another, 94.9 percent of the pollutant. By 1961, this proportion had reached 96.7 percent, and by 1965, it had reached 98.9 percent.

In the typical TSP manufacturing plant, once the level of engineering control efficiency (the ratio of input fluorides *not* emitted to total input fluorides) gets much above 95 percent, the attainment of further control efficiency becomes extremely expensive and, in some of the older plants, impossible. As a practical matter, sources of phosphate rock having lower fluoride content were unavailable. Thus, only two basic control alternatives were available to the phosphate companies. Either they could adjust production processes so that greater quantities of fluorides would be present in the fertilizer output, or they could install further specialized equipment to recover larger quantities of the liberated fluorides. The major means of recovering fluorides is by spraying water into the gas streams containing the pollutant, which in turn creates a problem of pollution in the spray water.

Some studies of the costs of air pollution control in phosphate plant operations have indicated that 95 percent to 96 percent control is virtually the maximum possible for plants built during the early 1950s. A plant built during the late 1950s had to spend $350,000 to increase its control efficiency from 97 percent to 98 percent, and an additional $350,000 to raise the control from 98 percent to 98.6 percent. To go from 98.6 percent to 99 percent required another investment of $525,000 on production process changes and control equipment. The next notch from 99 percent to 99.2 percent involved another $400,000. In other words, control costs increased at a much faster rate than the control itself. Through 1959, the phosphate companies had invested 6.7 million dollars to achieve a control efficiency of about 95 percent. Between 1959 and 1966, this same set of plants had invested an additional 16 million dollars to increase control efficiency to 99 percent (phosphate company figures).

Given the apparently extreme cost of achieving levels of

control in excess of 99.5 percent, it obviously became worthwhile for the companies to follow the land purchase option after achievement of this level. By 1964, the companies had increased ownership of nonurban land by almost 80 percent within the quarter million acres the State of Florida declared to be subject to pollution damages. Some of this land was leased back to cattlemen and citrus growers, mostly the former, at rather low prices and with a clause exempting the companies from fluoride damage liability. Unfortunately, these land purchases were to little avail, for in 1966 the state imposed emission standards closely approximating the previously mentioned feasible technological minimums. The imposition of these standards obviously removed the incentive for the companies to purchase more land for fluoride disposal purposes. The market recognized this change and premiums were no longer paid for land within the polluted area.

Imposing emission standards seemed to have served little if any economic purpose. The shift in property rights in the air resource from the phosphate companies to the cattlemen and growers, occurring under the land purchase option, fully compensated cattlemen and reduced damages to growers. The land purchase option changed the specification of property rights as far as who had to pay whom to modify the air resource used for disposal. The phosphate companies became generators of waste; at the same time, they became major owners of pasture and citrus lands. This arrangement forced them to act simultaneously as emitters and receptors. Thus, they chose that combination of processes and resulting emissions which minimized the sum of damage control costs, damage costs, and administrative costs. They continued to maximize their return from the air resource just as they had prior to the land purchase option, but they could no longer treat this resource as a free good. Now they had to realize that by emitting fluorides into the atmosphere they were imposing costs on themselves. Now they had to maximize their joint returns from phosphate *and* land. This arrangement resulted in a lower level of emissions than had existed prior to the option arrangement. In other words, with the shift in the responsibility for initiating bargaining, the outcome changed.

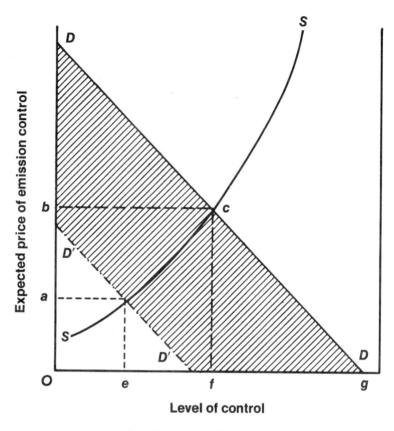

Figure 5.1   Market for Fluoride-free Air in Polk County

Notice that the imposition of emission standards meant that land, particularly pasture land, was no longer being used for its most valuable purpose, fluoride disposal, but rather as pasture land, which the market valued substantially less.

Let's return for a moment to our graphics. Figure 5.1 presents a simplified picture of our Polk County situation. The graph shows the control cost curve of the phosphate companies as a supply of clean air (SS). Notice that it is a *line* rather than a band, indicating that the uncertainty, and thus *ICP* costs, facing the emitters was zero. They knew what it would cost them to clean up the air. This, of course, is an overstatement of the case. Notice also that this supply curve increases expo-

110

nentially (bloody fast) as high levels of control are attained. This represents the facts as we have just described them; namely, that each extra percentage of air cleanliness is more expensive than the previous one. The demand for clean air (*DD*) shows the maximum demand, given zero *ICP* costs. Since demanders were subjected to high levels of uncertainty, *DD* consisted of a band (*DDD'D'*). Given property rights vested in the emitters, the effective demand curve they faced is given by *D'D'*. Therefore a clean air level of *oe* occurred at an expected price of *oa*.

Alternatively, vesting the property rights in the receptors meant that demanders were no longer faced with the uncertainty and the high *ICP* costs of the previous case. Since emitters now had to initiate bargaining and to recognize the total costs of their actions, the expected control price rose to *ob* and the level of control rose to *of*.

The outcome changed, because the initiation of bargaining responsibility was shifted from the parties with relatively *high ICP* costs (cattlemen and growers) to the parties with relatively *low ICP* costs (the companies). The change in the *law* changed the economics. Receptors no longer had to bear the *ICP* costs of searching out the causes of damages, of identifying perpetrators, and of assuring participation of the hundreds of receptors who would benefit from emission reductions. Nor did they have to consider, in deciding about a proposed bargain, the expected costs of policing such a bargain. Receptor *ICP* costs now consisted of the relatively minor fees for real estate transfer and for information on emitter control costs. Emitter *ICP* costs, in addition to real estate transfer fees, now consisted of the comparatively easy task of getting the ten or eleven companies to determine what combination of land purchases and emission cutbacks would be cheapest. Also, the receptor lands within the pollution area had to be identified. Once this was done and land purchases were made, the costs faced by the companies were the same as those faced by any joint production activity. These costs did *not* involve guesses about levels of emissions, because they knew perfectly well what the levels would be. Neither did they have to worry about policing an agreement, because they owned the land themselves. The control district no longer served any useful purpose, because emission of fluorides by the companies would damage only the companies. The shift in the property rights increased the value of the services yielded by the air resource without reducing the value of services from any other resources. This net gain resulted because the sum of damage and damage control costs were reduced, as was the cost of necessary transactions and exchanges. Basically, the shift in property rights made economically possible exchanges that had not previously been worthwhile. Reduced *ICP* costs caused a change in the outcome—reduced air pollution.

6
CHAPTER

Controlling
The Crud

In Chapter 4 we made the point that because different systems of property rights are associated with different levels of *ICP* costs, environmental outcomes under the many possible property rights systems differ as well. Effective *ICP* costs vary with different property right assignments. Similarly, exchange possibilities and market outcomes can change with changes in the configuration of property rights. In Chapter 5 we presented a "real world" example in which a change in the distribution of rights did, in fact, affect exchange possibilities and the resulting environmental quality.

All attempts to improve environmental quality are basically modifications of the property rights that exist at the time. The range of individual discretion in the use of environmental resources is broadened or narrowed in accordance with the way in which *ICP* costs decrease or increase. The implication is that the environmental quality problem is basically a problem of finding the optimal set of constraints on individual discretion for each situation. This further implies that there is *no unique universal solution* to these problems, since *ICP* costs can differ drastically according to:

1. The attributes of the resource involved.
2. The attributes of its users.
3. The uses to which the resource is to be put.

For example, if one is interested only in one or two attributes of an air mass, and these attributes remain relatively stable over time, then the use of a fee simple absolute system will probably not create excessive informational costs. On the other hand, if complete specification of the atmosphere is required, many of these attributes can be specified only *conditionally*. If the temperature is *x*, the particulate capacity is *y*, and so on. In this case, the informational costs associated with the fee simple absolute system is excessive, to say the least. It then becomes necessary to resort to some alternative property rights system that limits individual discretion to a larger extent. Thus, there is no "unique" property rights system that will produce "the" solution to the environmental quality problem. "The" is used in the sense that it is simple and universally acceptable. All these systems have costs and benefits associated with them, and these costs and benefits for a given system will vary from situation to situation. The problem is to identify that system which is most suitable for a *given* situation.

Unfortunately, very little is known about the systematic behavior of *ICP* costs. Ideally, we should be able to recount (1) for a given situation, how *ICP* costs will vary with different property rights systems, and (2) for a given property rights system, how *ICP* costs vary over situations. In Chapter 4, our discussion centered on the second of these topics—one property right system, the fee simple absolute. We discussed how the level of *ICP* costs associated with the fee simple absolute differed among various types of valuable resources. In this chapter, we will discuss in a strictly qualitative way how *ICP* costs in a given situation seem to vary with various property right configurations. The specific situation is again drawn from air pollution, although most of what we say applies equally to other environmental quality problems. We cannot hope to pick out all the factors of a given pollution problem which contribute to *ICP* costs, although we will give attention to the major ones.

Again, we will use the Polk County air pollution case from

the previous chapter. Although this example is less complex than is found in a typical urban air pollution case, the difference is one of degree rather than kind. Let us go back to 1957 and assume that we have been hired by the State of Florida to suggest a course of action to resolve Polk County's problems. Obviously, things have been getting worse and there is no relief in sight. Several additional companies have even announced their intention to open up new TSP plants in the area. We have been told *secretly* that our job is to maximize the efficiency of Polk County's air resource use. We have also been told *secretly* not to concern ourselves with the income distribution effects, since local tax policy will handle that item. The secrecy is required because the state official cat who gave us the job didn't want to be accused of giving those damnyankee (one word) phosphate companies a "license to pollute." Neither did he want to be threatened with a mass exodus of the companies if their emissions were to be restricted in any way. We are charged with finding the *instrument* that will minimize the sum of all parties' costs—*ICP*, damage, and emission control.

As would-be controllers of Polk County's air pollution, we recognize that there are a wide variety of ways in which control can be exercised. Nevertheless, all these ways fall into three more or less distinct classes:

1. Direct bargaining between sufferers and perpetrators.
2. Use of taxes or subsidies.
3. Use of rules and regulations.

Obviously, combinations of these classes are also possible. The first alternative involves the voluntary exchange of *bundles of rights* in situations where all parties are willing and able to bargain. The second consists of having a central body of one sort or another set a price on certain forms of perpetrator activity to make it economically "worthwhile" for them to act some specific way. In the third alternative, the control body simply decides for itself which activities of sufferers and perpetrators are worthwhile, and then formulates rules and regulations that sufferers and perpetrators must obey or else be subject to penalties. This approach differs from the tax subsidy alternative in that the *legal* choices available to the parties are severely limited. The tax subsidy approach still legally allows alternatives, although the cost of such choices may be high.

After looking the situation over in some detail, it is fairly obvious that there is little likelihood of a voluntary bargaining solution under the existing configuration of property rights. The two most common means of achieving voluntary solutions are *bribes* and *mergers*. Neither seems to be particularly practical for Polk County. The several hundred cattlemen and citrus growers might have come together and worked out some method of bribing a phosphate company to decrease or discontinue fluoride emissions. As we presented in Chapter 3, if the amount of the necessary bribe is less than the damages imposed on the farmers, the farmers will be better off paying the bribe. Of course, the farmers would never offer a bribe larger than their damages, since it would then be cheaper to suffer such damages. The phosphate companies, in turn, would accept or reject the bribe in accordance with their own best self-interests. If the bribe was larger than the cost of controlling emissions to the required level, accept it they would and emissions would be reduced. If their costs exceeded the value of the bribe, they would merely reject it. In any case, a *quantitative measure* of the damages suffered by the farmers would have been made clear to the companies. Because of the possible revenue from the bribe, the companies could no longer ignore the effects of their emissions. *Acceptance* of the bribe would indicate that the companies were at least as well off as before. If the transaction takes place at all, one side must have been made at least slightly better off. Once trading stopped, *further* transaction would benefit one party *only* at the expense of the other. Of course, if the companies reject the bribe, the value to them of using the air as a waste disposal medium is greater than the value of damages suffered by the farmers.

Unfortunately, for reasons covered in the last chapter, it is unlikely that any bribe would actually be offered. The damages suffered by the individual farmer are difficult to calculate, and thus the proper share of each farmer's contribution to the bribe is uncertain. Most farmers would probably realize that if they *didn't* contribute while others did, they could gain benefits without cost (free rider). If all farmers figure this out, no bribe will be available. Finally, an intelligent bribe requires knowledge on the part of the farmers about alternative production methods and the emissions and costs associated with these methods so that companies could be prevented from cheating on any agreements. Suppose that after the bribe had been offered and accepted, the demand for *TSP* rises, thus generating increased output. The companies could now legitimately argue that a larger bribe would be required to maintain the agreed-upon level of emission. Unless the farmers knew their stuff about technology and costs, they could never be sure that the increased output was market created or merely blackmail. Again, a potentially useful control instrument is marred by severe difficulties in its implementation.

Ruling out the solution by natural bribery, one more voluntary solution remains a possibility. Why not have a *merger* of cattlemen, growers, and phosphate companies? If these different types of enterprise could become one operation, the total operation would have to take account of all costs and benefits, including those among the different operations. The consolidated firm would balance the costs of reducing fluoride emissions from its phosphate division against the benefits such reduction would provide its citrus and cattle divisions. Profits would be maximized for the combined operation; maximization would, in turn, produce the same results of reduced pollution as the bribery case. For instance, the combined operation might calculate that reducing fluoride emissions by 10 percent would cost $1,000,000. They might also calculate that such a reduction would raise the net income of their citrus operations by $600,000 *and* the net income of their pasture operations by the same amount. In this case, they would be ahead of the game for their *total combined operation* to reduce the emission levels. These kinds of calculations would continue to be made to produce the combination of costs and outputs that would yield maximum net profit. The combine makes internally all trade-offs that will raise welfare. In this case, "welfare" is easily identified by combined net profit. This assumes, of course, that the firms had not been imposing other kinds of costs on one another prior to the merger.

A bit of investigation on our part, however, would show that under the existing system of property rights, neither sufferers nor perpetrators would have much incentive to attempt merger. Most of the difficulties of the bribery case are also present here. Both forming and implementing a merger would involve considerable cost. Free-rider problems would continue to exist. It is doubtful that any of the existing management personnel would have the expertise necessary to manage the diverse operations of citrus growing, cattle raising, and fertilizer production. This would further increase costs.

Phosphate companies could initiate a merger program themselves, but this wouldn't seem too worthwhile, given the existing property rights. Here again, though smaller numbers are involved, the free-rider problem could plague the companies' attempt to combine. If the companies increased their pollution levels, they might be able to drive down the price of the suffers' lands to a point that buying them up would be quite profitable. If the public ever found out about *this* little game of blackmail, the companies would really take it on the chin in the form of controls and sanctions. Finally, the U. S. Department of Justice would not look too kindly on a merger of the world's largest phosphate-manufacturing concerns. The courts would probably concur, since the industry has already lost several antitrust actions. Uncle Sam would probably (and correctly) maintain that the pollution control gains were not offset by the "substantial lessening of competition" that would occur under the merger scheme. He would probably tell the companies to solve the pollution problem some other way.

Well, that wipes out the probable usefulness of the voluntary alternatives, given the property rights system. Therefore, something has to be modified. To do that, there must be some organization other than one identified with the parties involved. This organization will at least have to decide the initial form and allocation of the air resource rights, and perhaps it will have to continue responsibility for such decisions. This body could be the courts, but more likely it will be some control group that has been virtually given the property rights to the resource. That is, the control agency has been given some discretion in deciding *how* the air is to be used, *who* can use it, and perhaps *whether or not* and *under what conditions* it can be sold.

For our problem we will assume that the great State of Florida has established such a control agency and assigned it the property rights to the air in question. We will further assume (for the moment) that the personnel of this agency is willing to allocate the air rights in a manner consistent with *economic efficiency* criteria.

Even a brief review of the means employed by most air pollution control agencies shows that their favorite has been the rules and regulation route. There exist an almost limitless number of possible rules and regs, but only a few have ever been used or suggested.

The most common suggestion for a regulation made by sufferers and their assorted friends is the *outright prohibition* of all emissions of all pollutant materials. Proposals such as this are implied by statements that *any* waste-generating activity which damages a single human life or interferes with one other man's enjoyment of his property must be prohibited. In the Polk County case, such a regulation would mean that the companies couldn't emit *any* fluorides, growers couldn't protect their crops from frost, and cattlemen couldn't employ insect control programs. Frost and insect control also generate air pollution. It would also mean that the locals would have a helluva time with mosquitoes. Polk County would probably have cleaner air (how about the swamp gas?), but nobody except a few swamp rats, alligator poachers, and bear hunters would be around to enjoy it. It would be *prohibitively* expensive to eliminate *all* pollutants. Anyway, the atmosphere does have some ability to dilute and assimilate waste materials. There's no justifiable economic reason why this ability should not be used.

By far the most frequent type of regulation favored by control agency administrators is the *standard*. Local, state, and federal air pollution laws are full of talk about emission, ambient, and input standards. *Emission standards* specify either the maximum quantity of a pollutant to be released into the atmosphere over some time period or the maximum allowable concentration of a pollutant in some stream of waste materials. *Ambient standards* specify the maximum concentration of pollutant material that may exist in the atmosphere. *Input standards* specify either the types of inputs an emitter may use or the manner in which he may use these inputs. Thus the emission and input standards are a means of achieving coordination between the waste discharges of individual emitters, while the ambient standard represents the level of air quality desired.

The discussions that follow are a bit tedious. Part of this tedium may be caused by the writing style, but a good part of it comes from the simple fact of life that we're talking about a whale of a lot of factors all at the same time. It's like the juggler with ten bottles in the air. Drop one, and the whole rhythm is knocked out of whack. So bear with the apparent redundancies and repetitions. There just ain't no simple way to get through these bloody important concepts. So here we go.

Once the crud has been dumped into the air by the phosphate companies, it is dispersed in a way that will be determined by the meteorological conditions, the configuration of the surrounding terrain, and the specific form of the fluorides themselves. Therefore, a given emission will affect various farmers differently in time and space. Each separate plant will have a pattern of emission damages that will differ from other plants. Even the same plant will damage its neighbors in differing degrees depending on weather conditions, the location of the neighbors, and the characteristics of production in the plant at the given time. In addition, control costs for similar amounts of emissions are likely to differ among plants because of minor differences in their production processes. Strictly optimal allocation of Polk County's air resource requires separate calculation of cost benefits for each emitting plant. These calculations would have to consider each *set* of emitter cost savings and receptor damage costs associated with all conceivable sets of meteorological and production conditions. Different emission standards would be required for *each plant* and for *each set of conditions,* if the sum of emitter costs and receptor damages is to be continuously minimized. In other words, the number of "tailored" emissions standards under each set of conditions must approach the number of emitters. If there are a fair number of sets of conditions, the number of emitter standards will be greater than the number of emitters. Emission standard calculation would be a formidable task indeed, or so it would appear.

The achievement of this minimum aggregate sum by means of input standards requires even *more* information than emission standards. We would still need to know everything we had to know before. In addition we would have to figure out what combination of inputs brings about what levels of emissions. For example, assume an emission standard for a particular plant can be met by some combination of low fluoride content rock and TSP storage time *or* some combination of sulfuric and phosphoric acid use. The control agency must know which combination is the least costly for that particular plant. Since the quality of the plant's output will also be affected by the choice of inputs, the agency must also know the characteristics of the demand for the plant's products in addition to the costs of its inputs. Absence of such knowledge might mean that costs are being imposed on the phosphate companies for which there is no corresponding gain in pollution control.

A special case of the emission standards approach which has had great appeal is the equiproportionate abatement rule. Application of this rule would appear to be an "equitable" arrangement in rationing out the disposal abilities of the air resource. The rule would require that all companies reduce their emissions by some fixed proportion of their historical level. The same percentage decrease would be required of all plants. Sounds fair, equitable, and economical, right? Wrong again! In the first place, if we're going to try this kind of stunt, we'd better keep our mouths shut or the plants will really start pouring out the crud in grand style. If *future* emissions are going to be based on past history, the companies are going to try and make that history as cruddy as possible.

Most important, as economists, we'd really be out of our tree if we accepted this concept. If all the plants were identical, and the cost to each was identical to achieve a given percentage reduction, no sweat. Our equiproportionate rule would be the same as the cost of reduction situation. We've already pointed out, however, that our Polk County plants varied greatly in their age and the costs each would incur in reducing pollution by a given proportional amount. Even more important than this, those plants which had already tried to do something about the problem—had in fact reduced their emission levels—would probably face very high costs for further reductions compared to other plants which had done nothing in the past. Thus, we would be rewarding the bums that hadn't done anything and penalizing those companies that had. The fact that control costs increase rapidly for control levels over 95 percent adds weight to this argument. In addition to its being "unfair," the rule also violates economic efficiency, which dictates that the least cost abatement be carried out for the total desired reduction in pollutants. Plants which have the least cost of reducing emissions should in fact be carrying out these reductions. Similar points can be made against *any* rule or regulation applied across the board without regard for differences among emitters in the damage costs they cause or the control costs they must bear.

An alternative to the use of standards set by the agency is the *setting or influencing of prices.* If the agency is to have *perfect information* at all times, it would make no difference whether it used rules and regulations or set prices. The outcome would be the same in either case. The standard would be set so that the sum of control costs and damage costs would be minimized. Similarly, the agency could set a price on emissions so that the plants would voluntarily choose that level of emissions which minimized the aforementioned sum. Again, assuming *perfect information,* the only apparent reason for price setting instead of rules and regulations involves financing. If the form of the price setting is the use of an *effluent charge* —so many dollars per ton of crud released—then the control agency can finance its operations from the receipts. If the flow of funds from the effluent charge replaces funds from the public treasury, it is possible to reduce taxes and other sources of government revenue. Some of these taxes, such as excise taxes on positive goods, are known to have negative effects on economic efficiency. Thus, an effluent charge could conceivably increase the efficiency with which the environment is used, at the same time reducing inefficiencies elsewhere caused by government tax programs.

If information available to the control agency is either

costly or imperfect, the pricing alternative probably has some other advantages as compared to the emission standard. Whether the price is an effluent charge or a subsidy to cleanup efforts, if it is based on additional damages caused by additional emissions, it requires only knowledge of the receptors' damage function. Thus, in the Polk County case, we would have to know only the value of crop and cattle damages caused by each plant to calculate the minimum sum of damage and control costs. The reason is because the plant will continue to emit *only* as long as the gain from additional emitting exceeds that which it can receive (subsidy or bribe) or that which it has to pay to reduce emissions. The emitter is the only one that needs to know the control costs, if the effluent charge or subsidy payment is based on *additional* receptor damages. Of course, since receptor damages are usually very difficult to determine, the real advantage of the price in this case is small. The difference is comparable to the alternatives of drowning in the Atlantic or drowning in the Pacific.

Price setting does have one distinct advantage over *input standards,* although emission standards have the same advantage. A set price means that if the emitter can find a cheaper way of attaining the same reduced output of crud, he'll be able to pocket the savings. Therefore, there is an incentive to reduce emission and/or reduce the costs of control. Emissions standards provide incentives for reducing the cost of a given level of crud production, but does not necessarily encourage lower emissions *per se.* However, the *input standard* locks a plant into a technological straitjacket. It gives no incentive to look for lower cost methods of control. It also provides no incentive for reducing levels of pollutant emission. The plants' flexibility in choosing their own least-cost control methods is completely destroyed. The only way an inputs standard would be "best" is if the control agency knew better than the phosphate companies which method of control was cheapest for each separate producing unit.

One form of pricing particularly appealing to emitters is to pay or subsidize the companies for *not* emitting fluorides. Implicit in this approach is the idea that the companies possess the fee simple absolute property rights to the entire atmosphere. Since it is costly for cattlemen and growers to form a group to deal with the companies, the control agency performs this function for them, using public funds.

Subsidies can take several forms. One more common form is the suggestion that accelerated depreciation be allowed to companies who purchase certain types of air pollution devices. In effect, this amounts to an interest-free loan to the companies, since they can take the money saved from potential present tax payments and earn interest on it. Of course, the total depreciation allowed over time is the same, but assuming the companies are making money, this early write-off gives them the use of the money sooner. Clearly, under this type of subsidy, the emitter has a strong incentive to qualify as much of his equipment as possible for the pollution control consideration. Since equipment in a given process is integrated to a greater or lesser extent, the distinction between pure pollution control equipment and straight production equipment is not always clear.

A variation on the accelerated depreciation theme is the proposal that emitters be granted a tax credit for control equipment they purchase. This differs from the depreciation scheme in that the credit constitutes a *flat deduction* from the emitter's tax bill. If, for example, a 20 percent credit is given for the purchase of pollution control equipment, the emitter may deduct 20 percent of the purchase price of the machine *from his tax bill* in the year of the purchase. Obviously, this amounts to a 20 percent reduction in the cost of the pollution control device. The government picks up the tab for this portion.

Other forms of governmental subsidies to perpetrators exist, although the preceding two are the ones most commonly suggested. Governments give grants and contracts for research, development, and demonstration projects. Some areas exempt pollution control equipment from excise and property taxes. It is even conceivable that governments might make outright payments to pollution emitters. Ideally, these payments would equal those which sufferers *would have made* had they not had to contend with the costs of forming a coalition. Thus, they would be equal to the residual damages faced by sufferers after having made all economically feasible adjustments to existing pollution.

Understandably, emitters are all for as many subsidy payments as they can get. They have several arguments or threats with which to plead their cases. One more popular argument is that pollution control equipment is "nonproductive." Therefore, why should emitters be required to finance such equipment? The implication is that the atmosphere is somehow different in economic principle than any other scarce input, such as labor or phosphate rock. Of course, the phosphate firms employ labor and phosphate rock because they are the cheapest means of producing their fertilizer. Firms have to *pay* for these inputs only because the inputs have valuable alternative uses. Similarly, firms use the atmosphere because it is the cheapest means of ridding themselves of the waste products from their production processes. The atmosphere also has valuable uses for the cattlemen and growers which they are willing to pay for. Economic theory as well as just plain horse sense tells us that firms will use any input which increases the difference between revenues and costs. The emitter's use of the atmosphere contributes to this maximization of profit just the same way as does labor, phosphate rock, or presumably the "nonproductive" Cadillac limo of the plant's general manager.

The argument that pollution control efforts are nonproductive really means that such efforts are nonproductive from the point of view of the perpetrator. The efforts are *very* productive from the viewpoint of sufferers—in this case, cattlemen and growers. The phosphate companies don't want to bear the costs of control when the farmers are going to be the beneficiaries. In other words, the companies don't like the implicit assignment of air property rights to the sufferers. Clearly, they would prefer that the sufferers pay them not to pollute. Companies feel that *they* should have the air property rights.

If the companies are not very successful in arguing the righteousness of their cause, they may adopt another tactic—the threat that increased costs of pollution control will drive them out of business, thus lowering incomes and creating unemployment in Polk County. For some of the older and less efficient plants, this is probably true. These plants previously disposed of their waste by dumping it into the air and telling it to go away. If some plants are made to adopt control measures, they will find their expense exceeding their revenues and they will be forced out of business. Since people generally are loath to see local unemployment or decreases in incomes—even temporary—this argument is likely to carry great weight in the community. Basically, however, the argument revolves around another question. Can the phosphate plant meet all the costs of producing its output? In the past, the plants produced fertilizer and sold it at a price which covered all costs *except waste disposal.* The waste disposal costs were being borne *involuntarily* by cattlemen and growers. In this situation, had the industry expanded until the least profitable plant was just breaking even, any new costs would have forced some closings. Total costs would have exceeded total revenues for the least efficient plants, which would have had to abandon operations. In other words, given waste disposal costs, the total cost of producing fertilizer in these plants is greater than the price consumers of phosphate fertilizers are willing to pay. A subsidy merely means that the government is willing to trade off economic inefficiencies in production of fertilizer so that Polk County's workers, residents, and phosphate companies do not have to move their resources to new locations and/or occupations.

Pollution sufferers are likely to make similar arguments for imposing an effluent charge instead of paying a subsidy. Receptors will most likely argue that the pollution they are suffering is *counterproductive*; that they are being forced to bear costs for which they receive no benefits; and that unless relief is forthcoming, they will be forced out of business, with similar detrimental effects on the local economy. The proper replies to these sufferer arguments are the same as those given to the perpetrators when discussing subsidies. However, the implicit assignment of air rights to sufferers through the effluent charge has some advantages over the implicit assignment of air rights to perpetrators through the subsidy program.

First, a subsidy increases the burden on funds from the public treasury. Usually, the burden is born by the general taxpayer instead of the sufferers and their customers. Farmers are receiving a volume of clean air which does have valuable alternative uses, but they have paid nothing for this use—the taxpayer has paid. With the air rights implicitly vested in the companies, a customary market arrangement with negligible *ICP* costs would mean that *sufferers* would pay the perpetrators not to pollute. This would force them to account for the air's valuable alternative uses in their production activities. But with a taxpayer-paid subsidy, the farmers can now regard the air as a free good. This means that they will use *more* of it than would be optimal under a market arrangement, and their attempted production will be *larger* than under a market solution. The taxpayer is subsidizing both fertilizer production and beef/citrus production. Only if the subsidy received by the phosphate plants is collected as taxes from the sufferers (proportionally to their damages) and only if farmers recognize the specific purpose for which the tax is collected will this bias be avoided. Economic efficiency can be attained *if and only if* perpetrators find it worthwhile to recognize as a cost to themselves the costs their activities impose on others. Similarly, sufferers must count as their own costs the opportunities their activities take from others.

A second difficulty with the subsidy occurs when part of the subsidy is based on the perpetrator's control cost rather than wholly on the sufferer's damage costs. In this case, any reduction in control costs would in turn reduce the subsidy paid. This setup tends to reduce incentives for improving control technology and efficiency. However, it would have a substantial impact only if the subsidy covered *all* control costs. Partial subsidies merely reduce emitter-viewed "losses" from control efforts. They do not make these efforts "profitable." Partial subsidies based on control costs can impart a bias to results when they apply only to equipment used to capture end-product waste materials. Such payments reduce the cost of using "tail-end" equipment in relation to altering inputs or production processes, even though the latter may be the way of achieving least-cost control.

Most of the preceding discussion has assumed that our hypothetical control agency has been omniscient and clairvoyant. It is like the monkey in some Asian religion who knows all, sees all, hears all, and smells all without any effort whatsoever. Further, we have assumed that the agency can act instantaneously, costlessly, and without error when it receives its perfect information. Under these conditions, it makes little difference (usually) whether the body employs rules and regulations or subsidies and charges. All it need do is establish that set of emission/input standards or formulate that set of subsidies charges which will minimize the sum of *each* emitter's damage and control costs. Minimally, the agency's supernatural powers must be used to calculate the damages each emitter causes. However, two quite normal circumstances make this calculation logically impossible to perform. Under these circumstances, unique damages cannot be assigned to individual emitters who are part of a collection of emitters in a given area. These circumstances follow.

1. Whenever aggregate sufferer damages increase at a *faster rate* than increases in the level of pollution. For example, a citrus grower loses $100 per acre in the market value of his fruit in a year with some average emission of fluorides. If the emissions were to double, his damages might go to $300 per acre loss in fruit production, more than the proportional increase in the emission rate.

2. Whenever the pollution loadings in the air (or water, earth, or other element) are not the simple arithmetic sum of the contributions of individual emitters.

Figure 6.1a shows the relation described in point 1. Total emissions are plotted on the horizontal axis and total damages are plotted on the vertical axis. If damages were proportional to emissions, we would plot the relationship as a straight line, for example, C. Since damages increase at a faster rate than emissions, our function sweeps upward, as in C'. The three diagrams of Figure 6.1b illustrate point 2. If we get some pollutant "a" and plot the value of damage it causes, we obtain a line such as C_a. Taking pollutant "b" in the same environment produces a damage function such as C_b. If we dump both "a" and "b" into the environment at the same time, the damage is greater than would be the case for the sum of the separate damages (C_{a+b} is greater than $C_a + C_b$). This last phenomenon is called *synergism*. The damage of the sum of the two together is greater than that of the sum of the two separately.

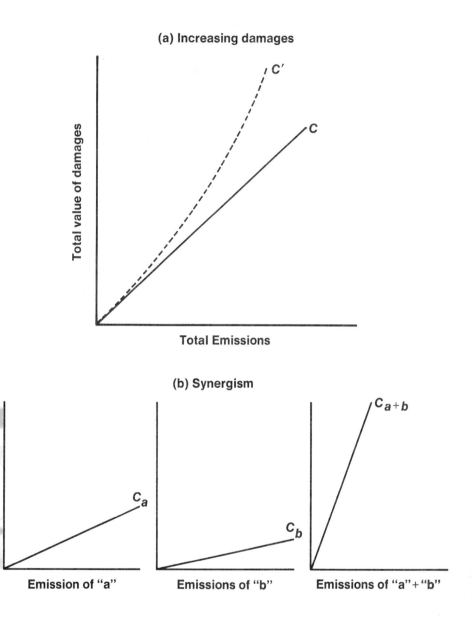

Figure 6.1 Damage Functions

Returning now to the requirement that damages increase proportionately with emission. If this is not the case, it is impossible to assign the responsibility for increased damages to any one emitter. The damage caused by this guy's emissions

129

is not just a function of his own emissions. The damage caused will also depend upon the emission level of the other polluters in the neighborhood. The damage he causes will be greater if *their* levels are greater, and vice versa. Thus, when total damages increase at a nonconstant rate, a change in the emissions of any one emitter can change the additional or incremental damages of all the others. This is true even though the emission levels of the others have stayed absolutely constant. Thus an emitter cannot know the emission conditions it will be worthwhile for him to meet unless he knows what the emissions of all other pollutant producers will be.

The problem becomes doubly impossible when chemical reactions take place in the air or watercourse that change the characteristics of the two or more pollutants mixed in the resource. If the resulting damages are greater than the arithmetic sum of the two combined, how does one assign the damage? The answer is "arbitrarily." There ain't no other way.

In Polk County, the synergism problem does not appear to exist with regard to the county's fluoride air pollution situation. It is not really known whether cattle and citrus damages increase at a constant rate. The few experiments performed do indicate that *nonlinearity* exists even when the variation in fluoride concentrations is very small.

Synergism and nonlinearity in damage functions have been shown to pose logically unresolvable problems for the control agency's job of centrally allocating the air resources of Polk County. As a practical matter, however, the agency's understandable lack of complete clairvoyance and omniscience prevent discovery of optimal damage and control costs sets. The effort and resources the agency would have to expend to calculate charges or rules that would minimize damage plus control costs would be phenomenal. Consider, for example, the task a control agency would face in calculating the damages to citrus groves caused by fluoride emissions of a single plant.

Even if the agency is able to determine what proportion of the fluorides deposited on a particular citrus site came from the plant in questions, its job has just begun. Fundamentally, the agency must determine these factors.

1. *The farmer's production possibilities.* This means *all* the production possibilities, not just those of using his given resources here and now. It includes production possibilities over time as well as at different places.

2. *The farmer's expectations about future production possibilities and future relative prices.* Included in this set of expectations is his expectation about future pollution levels.

3. *Finally, the farmer's feelings as to what he can afford to do.* Now consider this! If there are several substitutable production possibilities, and if each of these has several substitutable time and space dimensions, and if the owner and/or market expects these possibilities to change through time, and if there are several possible combinations of fluoride dosage concentrations and durations, *Then* the number of possible damage functions that must be considered by the control agency rapidly approaches astronomical dimensions. If the grove owner gets some nonmarket satisfactions out of owning the operation (like sitting in the shade under the old citrus tree), you're going to have to measure this phenomenon as well in order to be really accurate. In addition to being a phosphate plant engineer, chemist, atmospheric physicist, micrometeorologist, agronomist, horticulturist, statistician, and soothsayer, the control agency must also make like a psychoanalyst. To perform its duty properly, the agency would have to have a staff like that of a major university rather than a regulatory body with a severely limited budget.

Just for laughs, let's assume that the monumental job of calculating a specific grove owner's damage function has been accomplished according to the above outline. So what. We now have *one* grove owner's problem well identified *for this moment in time.* Unfortunately, this does not mean that we can apply these results to other grove owners as well. Too many of the parameters (variables) we determined apply only to our specific case. When we try to generalize the results to cover other grove operations, we're immediately in trouble. If you're really going to play this stupid game to get at some kind of scientific "truth," then you'll have to forget about economic rationality completely. This crazy route has been followed in many other fields many times before, so don't feel too bad if you get sucked into the same trap of insisting on *pure* "science" to obtain information.

We've already mentioned the business of technological synergism in which the sum of the damages caused by two mixed pollutants was greater than the sum of the damages each would have caused alone. There's an analogous problem in economic "synergism." Assume that all our growers were identical in their production possibilities and damage functions. One of the ways that each tries to adjust to the pollution problem is by substituting inputs. For example, a grower might try a less productive but more fluoride-resistant strain of tree. As long as just one grower tries this type of substitution, no sweat. His actions alone would not affect the relative prices of inputs enough to matter much. However, if all his neighbors and colleagues try the *same* substitution at the *same* time, they will affect and *affect plenty* the relative prices of inputs used to grow citrus. In short, the agency can't know the damages caused by a single *phosphate plant* unless it knows the effect of grower *interaction* as well as the actions of individual growers.

Finally, even if the agency accomplishes the superhuman job of establishing all the relations described above *at some point in time,* the bloody things probably won't be stable. All the work (or most of it) of yesterday ain't worth as much today, because someone changed the numbers and even the rules of the game. Think of all the "time-sensitive" factors involved. Age of trees, identities of owners, characteristics of property rights, input and output prices, technological innovations, expectations of all kinds—these can and will goof up the pretty little numbers so tediously obtained. If the agency really wants to determine a "true" damage function for each time period, the State of Florida had better stop all operations except the control agency. It will take all the resources of the state plus a bunch more besides. This operation might maximize something, but not overall social welfare. Agency investigators will make out like crazy, but they're the only ones. The costs of complete accuracy far outweigh any gains due to complete minimization of damage plus control costs. A better criterion (if we wish to maximize *economic* efficiency) seems to be minimizing damage costs plus control costs plus *the* ICP *costs of all parties,* public and private.

If the agency took an alternative route and tried to determine the exact emission control functions for all the plants, its problem would be almost as bad. True, there are fewer plants than farmers, but each plant is at least slightly different from its neighbor, and the number of variables entering into the control function is still huge. Many of these variables change over time and space, as was the case for the receptor's damage functions.

By this time, if you're still awake, you should realize that the point of this whole section is to show the complete impossibility of any control agency's making its decisions based *just* on information and the scientific method. The *cost* of "science" in this case is just too damn high. The process is "informationally intensive," and the costs would skyrocket beyond belief if it were to be used in the strict sense described above.

As we have asserted, the whole point of establishing a control agency is to effectively reduce information, contracting, and policing costs. This is done by using some combination of property right assignments and/or performing some function which free markets had previously found too costly for some reason or another. Often, these reasons were based on *uncertainty* in one form or another. Fair enough. We've got our control agency, and we know *what* we want it to do (improve resource allocation), but we're still not sure just *how* it's supposed to do it. Let's look for a moment at the incentives acting on the members of the control agency before we press on with a suggestion or two.

You can be bloody sure that the agency's employees will know their own *ICP* costs pretty darn well. These are the costs that eat up the agency's budget, and it's that budget from which they get paid. The criterion we have asked the agency to use is the minimizing of receptor damage costs, emitter control costs, and everybody's *ICP* costs, including the government's (as represented by the agency). There are problems here that will only be noted in this tome. How de we provide incentives for the agency and its employees to do what we want? It's entirely possible that once a program had been implemented, it could continue to work without further agency action or supervision. If this be the case, our buddies in the agency are out of work. Given some choice in control instruments, what will encourage the agency to use the most economically efficient instruments as opposed to the most "agency-intensive" ones? There are no general answers for these questions any more than there are generalized answers to the pollution problem itself. But the *problem* of agency incentives must be recognized and dealt with on a case-by-case basis. Central responsibility removes many of the built-in controls of the market, and these controls must be replaced by something.

In practice, the usual incentives operating on a control agency have resulted in the use of *input* standards, which limit the inputs and processes an emitter may use. These input standards are often combined with *emission* standards, which limit the quantity of pollutants an emitter may release. Finally, these two standards are coordinated with an *ambient* standard, which limits the maximum concentration of pollutants allowed in the environmental resource involved. Control over input materials and equipment makes it technically unlikely that "excessive" pollutants will be generated. Emission standards reinforce the input standards. Both controls increase the agency's predictability of the pollution level. They also make it possible for the agency to spot-check the situation rather than monitor it continually. The latter would be essential for any system of effluent charges or effluent subsidies. Thus, this method reduces substantially the agency's policing costs as compared to price-setting alternatives. The spot-checks will be effective as long as the penalties for noncompliance are substantial. Even if the chances of being caught are fairly remote, if penalties for being caught are high enough, intermittent policing should suffice.

The standards proposed by most control agencies for the environmental resource are usually based on human health criteria. These levels usually approximate those which will not harm the most susceptible person in the population concerned. Sometimes, as in the case of Polk County, the criteria are based on harm to things as well as humans, and the damage threshold is even lower than the human tolerance. Ambient standards are only objectives. They are statements of what the agency *hopes* to accomplish, or at least what the agency wants the taxpayers to *think* is the objective. Generally, the agency wants to approach this level gradually to prevent "undue" stress on the emitters.

Often, both the standard and the time schedule to achieve it are based not on objective criteria but on interminable haggling between emitters and the controlling body. The outcome often contains a high degree of arbitrariness, although the haggling tends to keep it to a minimum. In a way, the haggling is a substitute for the more costly calculation of optimal standards. Of course, while all this is going on, the public can be led to believe that all is well, particularly if the agency has funds for providing its public with "information." "Special exceptions" from the rules are also likely to crop up with increasing frequency as each emitter is allowed to present his heartrending tale of woe to the dirty old control agency. Meanwhile, the lags created by negotiation may mean that final controls may be put on an environment that no longer exists. The problem may be very different indeed than when the discussions started.

By itself, no control procedure involving *continuous central control* of Polk County's air resource seems to have much to recommend it. No presently conceivable control agency can realistically pretend to be capable of making the same decisions that emitters and receptors *would have made* in a market where *ICP* costs were negligible. Nor does resorting to bilateral negotiations between the agency and emitters offer a satisfactory alternative. In practice, it is unlikely that the interests of receptors will be sufficiently represented. Regulatory and/or exchange services must also be economized, as well as the resource in question. Therefore, the ideal is seldom if ever attainable, and we must fall back on some "second best" solutions.

There is an alternative to continuous control agency allocation. The air rights of Polk County are now vested in the agency. The agency would define the rights in terms of allowable emissions, and then peddle these emission rights on a competitive basis. The emission standards might even allow for differing weather conditions at different times. The problem of high receptor *ICP* costs remains, however, in determining a rational price. Emitters don't have too much of a problem, but the poor old sufferers *still* have a devil of a time getting information on which to base their bids. As a result, the emitters would again have a major advantage in bidding for the air rights. Just because we have the control agency selling the rights doesn't mean that we have lowered *ICP* costs for any of the other parties. With this in mind, let's look at one workable solution to the specific problem at hand. Notice, we've said *one* solution to the *specific* problem. If you get nothing more than this idea from this book, our success is assured! *There is no unique solution for the overall pollution problem.*

Several mathematical models are around which can be used to simula⁺e the transport and diffusion capacities of the atmosphere. Remember, it is the scarce diffusion and assimilative capacities of the atmosphere that we wish to allocate efficiently. Although these models are somewhat different, each model describes the probabilities of pollution dosages and durations that would exist, given a wide variety of emission sources, weather conditions, and topography. When the models are programmed for computers, one can play around with the various input variables to obtain probability estimates of what's going to happen under many combinations of input factors. This proposal would use such a model to establish ambient air standards which would specify pollution levels that could never be exceeded more than some given proportion of the time. If desired, the standard could vary from area to area within the county; but within any one area, no change in the standard would be allowed except perhaps at regular intervals of substantial duration. The *standard* is being used as a means of saving resources that would otherwise have been spent searching for information.

Based on the standard, emission rights would be established. The size of these rights in terms of the allowable pollution would be determined by reference to the values calculated from the model. These rights would then be put up for competitive bidding by the control agency. Anybody—receptor, emitter, collective bodies, conservationists, or speculators—could bid for them. Rights would be transferable from location to location as long as no specific location's ambient air standard was exceeded. Thus, a locational transfer could take place when unused capacity existed in the new location. It could also take place whenever the transferor compensated holders of existing rights for the reduction of their allowable emissions. The property rights established in the atmosphere with this approach are conditional and are based on probabilities about the state of the environment, present and future.

Consider what would happen under this system if, for simplicity, a uniform ambient air standard was established over our problem area. We will assume that we're able to define some unit of pollution, like pounds of fluoride per hour, that gives us a unit with which to describe the air right. Those subareas with the greatest assimilaitve capacities would have the greatest number of emission rights, simply because they are capable of handling a greater volume of waste before the ambient standard is exceeded. The availability of the greater number of rights means that, with a given demand, the price of the rights will be lower in that area. This further implies that everything else being equal, emitters will tend to locate in this high dilution/assimilation area until its ambient air standard is about to be exceeded. Again assuming demand to be constant, emitters would then tend to settle in areas having the next greatest emission rights, and so on and on. It's the same ball game as with agricultural land. In this case, the most productive land feels the first bite of the plow. For our problem, areas with the greatest waste disposal capacity would be the first to feel the raunchy breaths of the smokestacks.

If the demand for emission rights increased, two things would occur. First, the value of the emission rights in all areas would increase, but the value in the high-capacity area would increase more. Firms for which waste disposal represents a substantial portion of their total costs will tend to locate in the high-capacity area to an even greater extent than before.

The preceding scheme closely resembles a zoning plan in which the waste disposal capacity of the atmosphere is the zoning criterion. The scheme specifies a range of acceptable conditions within which the market is allowed to optimize. The ambient standard sets absolute limits within which receptors and emitters must adjust.

The plan will produce prices which in turn will provide decision-making information. Knowledge of what everybody else is doing is less valuable than it was previously. Most of the information which otherwise would be required is embodied in the market price of the emission right. Individuals now have the vehicle by which to make optimizing adjustments of their own plans. Once the standard is established, no further information on damage costs or control costs is needed. The function of the control agency would be simply to police emissions to see that property rights are not being invaded. Given a system of substantial penalties for invasion of rights, occasional random spot-checks would deter most violators.

Perhaps the most important feature of this plan is the *certainty* about maximum emission levels and air pollution levels that the ambient air standard introduces. Now the expectations of both emitters and receptors are made similar, which means that the likelihood of a unique market price solution is greatly increased. Receptors will no longer have to employ flexible inputs with their inherent inefficiencies to prepare for contingent overdoses that may never occur. Emitters' uncertainty may also be reduced by having the price, instead of the whims of the control agency, allocate the rights. If the *cost* of preparing for contingencies is high, then the *return* to increased certainty will also be high. Contrary to those who feel that the effluent charge is a cure-all, the ambient air standard may *improve* economic efficiency if uncertainty has been large in the problem area. The scheme recognizes the trade-off to be had between continuous optimizing of costs and of damages and the reduction of uncertainty. *This is the key point.* More may be gained for the moment in environmental quality management by *reducing uncertainty* than by eternally searching for an ill-defined and almost unapproachable optimum. It is apparent that *ICP* costs are an important part of the system that determines this optimum; unfortunately, however, little is known at present about the theoretical properties or empirical behavior of these costs under various control strategies.

Much the same outcome could be obtained from straight-forward zoning. However, the competitive-bidding feature and the fact that rights to the air can be traded in a limited way between properties do have advantages. The competitive-bidding feature provides the control agency with a source of revenue with which to carry out its policing functions. Under a simple zoning system, these funds, were they to be derived from the air usage, would have to come from some kind of property tax which might well be allocatively inefficient.

The fact that the rights to air can be shifted among properties to a limited extent is attractive in that there may be zones where a shift within the zone will have no significant impact on the distribution of air pollution as simulated by the model. If *no* shifting is allowed, a new firm wishing to locate in a zone where no emission rights surplus existed might have to purchase an unwanted factory just to get the emission rights.

Obviously, this suggestion is no panacea. The main reason for presenting it here is to show that controls other than emission or input standards or emission prices can be very desirable, and may perhaps be required, in environmental quality control programs. The slightly modified zoning procedure outlined here is but one such possibility. Only recently have economists begun to take more than passing notice of the obvious fact that all aspects of voluntary exchanges are not necessarily embodied in the market price. That is, the value of all that is in fact exchanged is not always collapsed into the exchange price. Stipulations, both conditional and absolute, when made part of the market deal can substantially reduce *ICP* costs and the uncertainty which often generates them. To the extent that nonpecuniary controls reduce *ICP* costs, market operations can be improved. In short, it is not true that controls always inhibit the operation of markets. *They can also create markets.*

7
CHAPTER

The
End of
Crud

The title of this chapter refers to the end of this book, not the end of environmental quality problems. *That,* friends and neighbors, just ain't gonna happen as long as one man exists on earth who wants to stay here a little while before his body joins the great crud pile of mother earth. A pessimistic view? Not really. It merely recognizes the facts of life as laid out in Chapter 2 about production, consumption, waste, and resources.

The fundamental question in environmental quality is how to get some of it. Many popular writings on the subject present issues in terms that encourage more slogans than understanding. In spite of the fact that nearly every human production and consumption activity generates waste, the issues are too often presented as some kind of holy war between filth purveyors and clean livers. Usually the villains are big and visible economic agents, like factories. The guilty ones are of course the faceless corporations that own these factories, and clearly, nobody cares if these fat cats suffer a bit anyway. Rhetoric pronouncing imminent threats to human survival gains greater acceptance. "Pure" environment is presented as "priceless" in that it is worth an infinite amount of time or other resources to attain. If this sort of approach gains the upper hand in policy formation, it would be possible to have environmental quality programs that would soon bring about and sustain something approximating a "pure" environment. But the victory, if one insists on calling it that, would not prove that anything of value had really come about. Rather, it would demonstrate that extremely rapid results can be achieved if one is willing to force others to make great sacrifices. Whether the results warrant the sacrifices is the basic economic question.

In any case, it is unlikely that the alternatives are quite so stark as the more excitable proponents of control would have everyone think. The major lesson economics teaches is that few if any environmental problems are of an either/or nature. The choice is nearly always one of a little more or a little less pollution. Even if there is a substantial improvement in the quality of the environment, the choice remains the same—a little more, or a little less, pollution. Furthermore, since *everyone* contributes to pollutant loadings—and also suffers from his and everyone else's contribution—*the problem belongs to everyone.* Its reduction requires some hard decisions about the individual and collective relations between men.

Many have been far too ready to accept shallow definitions of the causes of environmental quality deterioration. They have too often seen the essence of the problem as the presence of junk on the landscape, phosphates in the watercourses, or sulfur oxides in the atmosphere. Somewhat more perceptively, they sometimes view the problem as the escape of these pollutants from sewers and smokestacks. At one level of analysis, these *are* the causes of the problem. In another sense, however, they are only symptoms of the underlying causes. They are symptoms of human behavior as generated by the institutional rules of the game. While, to some extent, this is a matter of definition, it is *not* a matter to be settled arbitrarily. One's perspective does affect the action he chooses to take. The sewer viewed as a cause calls for an attack on the sewer. This is often the engineer's or technologist's response: put a control gadget on it. The difficulty is that this response overlooks any number of alternative actions, such as changing the locations of sufferers, having the perpetrator change his process, and other actions. It will almost certainly foreclose the possibility of attacking the real underlying cause—an absence of rules which make it worthwhile for perpetrators and sufferers to count as their own costs the costs they impose on others.

In practice, the environmental quality issue will probably depend on moral judgment that pollution is bad. The "bad" must be compared with other available alternatives, for example, reduced industrial activities with lower lowers of employment. Economic analysis can reduce these several alternatives espoused by different disciplines to a common and mutually understood measure of gains and losses. This result can be used to facilitate well-reasoned judgments about the relative efficacies of the alternatives. There are virtual libraries dealing with the physical, chemical, biological, and even legal aspects of environmental quality. Until recently, however, very little has been written dealing with the problem's economic aspects that did not take as a starting premise one or more absolute conditions; for example, we must clean the air, we must prevent any damages to human health, we must maximize gross national product. The reason for this lack is due to the analytical difficulties involved in both conceptualizing and testing the implied relations. However, emphasis cannot remain solely on what is scientifically or politically possible. *Some attention must be devoted to that which is economically possible as well.*

Throughout this book, the economically possible has been strongly identified with the availability of exchange possibilities. For a given set of production possibilities, greater exchange possibilities result in greater weights given to the decisions affecting others made by users of the environment. Exchanges take place through a market which under certain assumptions produces unique market prices or exchange ratios among the services provided by various commodities. When individuals place different values on environmental services, exchange continues until these different values are reconciled. In the absence of these exchange possibilities, opportunities for reconciliation, if they exist at all, are limited to rather rigid and tedious political processes where the intensities of individual preference are rarely registered accurately. The market can be viewed as a process in which the voluntary cooperation of many individuals establishes common values for similar services. For the last unit exchanged, everybody attaches the same value to a little more or a little less. The market consolidates all the available knowledge of owners about alternative uses and ensures the resource's use in ways that will maximize the difference between aggregate costs and aggregate benefits.

However, there ain't no such thing as a "free market." Markets are costly to produce, because their operation requires the existence of property rights. These rights must define with some precision permissible types of use, permissible exclusions, and permissible exchanges. If there are no property rights, there can be no exchange. The values of alternative uses are not revealed, because prices cannot be formed. Environmental services are consumed on a "fustest with the mostest" basis, and incentives to make investments in environmental improvements are lacking. It is axiomatic that all these problems in economic efficiency could be solved by a market in which definitive property rights were *established, exchanged, and enforced* without cost. If there were never any costs involved in obtaining information about the attributes of the goods in question, if actual transactions could be performed without effort, and if everybody were always completely honest, all the questions relating to economic efficiency would be automatically answered. The market would hear all, see all, and know all that was worth knowing, and would act to maximize the satisfactions obtained from environmental resources.

Often, however, complete individual discretion in the use of environmental resources involves such high *ICP* costs that a viable market is impossible. Now substantial divergences will separate the values different individuals attach to having a little more or a little less of a similar environmental resource. Modes of use will be biased, volumes of exchange will be reduced, and some of the advantages of specialized resource use will be lost to the community. Often the response to this situation is to vest the property rights in the resource in a central control agency which would then have the responsibility of finding the *equivalents* of markets without *ICP* costs. However, this is a pipe dream, because the costs of solving such a complex problem with so many changing factors would be staggering. This is particularly true when the agency isn't even staffed by persons capable of specifying the problem. There is no reason to believe that the divergences in values individuals attach to a little more or a little less will be any less under complete individual discretion about uses. Usually, some combination of control agency and individual discretion will serve to minimize *ICP* costs and thus maximize opportunities for exchange. But here is the key point. *No single combination* of factors will be universally applicable to environmental quality problems. *ICP* costs *vary* depending on the values of the multitude of variables present in each situation. Since these costs vary, the optimal way to minimize them will also vary. *There's no simple panacea!*

In summary, the basic question in environmental quality control is not of an either/or nature—a choice between complete centralized control and complete individual control. In most cases, these polar opposites are far too expensive. It is a question of the mix between private and central decision-making powers. The proportion must depend on the extent to which it can reduce uncertainty and enhance communication through exchange. The choice is not between two systems of control, one perfect and the other imperfect. The choice is between two imperfect systems, each of which has its own set of errors. It is necessary to do more than just test the two polar systems against some hypothetical supermarket system or supercommand system having zero *ICP* costs, and rejecting one if it doesn't measure up. Each situation will need a mix peculiar to its characteristics. The mix will probably be less than perfect. Compromise, baby. It's the name of the game, and the game is life itself.

Suggestions for Reading

This listing does not pretend to be all-inclusive of either topics or important research accomplishments in the economics of the environment. It is intended merely to point out some representative items the authors feel to be intelligible at the reader's level, while simultaneously providing some feel for technical possibilities and an overview of the economic–theoretic issues involved in environmental quality problems. A thorough understanding of environmental economics can be acquired only through an understanding of fundamental economic theory.

JOURNALS

Environmental Science and Technology. Contains general and technical articles on the chemical aspects of environmental quality, along with some discussion of policy issues.

Journal of Law and Economics. Much fundamental work dealing with the impact of property rights on economic behavior has appeared here.

Journal of the Air Pollution Control Association. Reports recent research in the basic sciences and technology of air pollution control. Gives some attention to policy issues. Each issue contains an extensive annotated bibliography of recently published works from all over the world.

Journal of the Water Pollution Control Federation. Provides up-to-date reports on recent research results in the basic sciences and technology of water pollution control. At least one issue each year reviews the past year's research accomplishments.

Natural Resources Journal. Devoted to the legal–economic aspects of natural resource problems.

Water Resources Research. Contains articles dealing with both the economics and the basic sciences and technologies of water resources.

BOOKS

Barnett, H. J., and C. Morse. *Scarcity and Growth.* Baltimore: Johns Hopkins University Press, 1963. Although its emphasis is on the quantity rather than the quality of natural resources, this book is absolutely fundamental to any serious study of natural resource problems.

Dales, J. H. *Pollution, Property, and Prices.* Toronto: University of Toronto Press, 1968. An engagingly written book which emphasizes the importance of property rights and *ICP* costs in environmental quality problems.

Davis, R. K. *The Range of Choice in Water Management.* Baltimore: Johns Hopkins University Press, 1968. A detailed engineering–economic study of water pollution control alternatives in the Potomac River estuary with emphasis on investment in control facilities.

Ely, R. T. *Property and Contract in Their Relation to the Distribution of Wealth.* Two volumes. New York: The Macmillan Company, 1914. A pioneering effort to establish the place of property right configurations in economic phenomena.

Kneese, A. V., and B. T. Bower. *Managing Water Quality: Economics, Technology, Institutions.* Baltimore: Johns Hopkins University Press, 1968. Presents interesting case studies of water pollution problems and discusses alternative means of control. Concludes that the effluent charge has the most desirable properties.

Mishan, E. J. *The Costs of Economic Growth.* London: Staples Press, 1967. An admittedly polemical piece which simultaneously stresses the place of property rights in the study of economic theory while questioning the manner in which much of this theory has been applied.

Ridker, R. G. *Economic Costs of Air Pollution.* New York: Frederick A. Praeger, Publisher, 1967. A first rigorous effort to establish the economic damages caused by air pollution.

ARTICLES

Boulding, K. E. "The Economics of the Coming Spaceship Earth," in H. Jarrett (ed.), *Environmental Quality in a Growing Economy*. Baltimore: Johns Hopkins University Press, 1966. Employs a successful imagery to present the materials balance concept.

Brown, G. M., Jr., and B. Mar. "Dynamic Economic Efficiency of Water Quality Standards or Charges," *Water Resources Research,* **4,** December 1968, pp. 1153–1159. Considers the impact of imperfect control agency clairvoyance on optimal control strategies.

Buchanan, J. M. "A Behavioral Theory of Pollution," *Western Economic Journal,* **6,** December 1968, pp. 347–358. Discusses the place of the free rider in environmental quality problems.

Cheung, S. N. S. "Transactions Costs, Risk Aversion, and the Choice of Contractual Arrangements," *Journal of Law and Economics,* **12,** April 1969, pp. 23–47. Stresses the relation between *ICP* costs, uncertainty, and the choice of exchange terms.

Coase, R. H. "The Problem of Social Cost," *Journal of Law and Economics,* **3,** 1960, pp. 1–44. The classic article in the theory of externalities. Stresses the neutrality of property right assignments with respect to the allocative efficiency of outcomes in the absence of *ICP* costs.

De Alessi, L. "Implications of Property Rights for Governmental Investment Choices," *The American Economic Review,* **59,** March 1969, pp. 13–24. Presents problems associated with centralized allocation of resources.

Demsetz, H. "The Exchange and Enforcement of Property Rights." *Journal of Law and Economics,* **7,** 1964, pp. 11–31. Points out that *ICP* costs inhibit the development of common values among individuals for a little less or a little more of similar resources.

Dolbear, F. T., Jr. "On the Theory of Optimum Externality," *The American Economic Review,* **57,** March 1967, pp. 90–103. Emphasizes the effect property right distributions can have on outcomes.

Gordon, H. S. "The Economic Theory of a Common Property Resource: The Fishery," *Journal of Political Economy,* **62,** April 1954. The seminal article in the analysis of common property rights.

Reich, C. A. "The New Property," *The Yale Law Journal,* **73,** April 1964, pp. 733–787. Warns of the dangers to individual freedom of vesting property rights in central bodies.

Subcommittee on Economy in Government of the Joint Economic Committee. *The Analysis and Evaluation of Public Expenditures: The PPB System.* (91st Congress, 1st Sess.) Washington, D.C.: Government Printing Office, 1969. Covers most aspects of the use of economic analysis in public decision making. The papers by Arrow and Steiner on market and nonmarket decision making, Kneese and d'Arge on environmental material balances, and Zeckhauser, Hirshleifer, and Shapiro on uncertainty are particularly worthwhile.

Wright, C. "Some Aspects of the Use of Corrective Taxes for Controlling Air Pollution Emissions," *Natural Resources Journal,* **9,** January 1969, pp. 63–82. Evaluates alternative pollution control instruments in terms of their informational requirements.